Donald Edgar

Donald Edgar, educated at Dulwich College and Oxford University, has been observing and writing about the royal family for over thirty years. After war service he had a notable career in Fleet Street as columnist, feature writer and foreign correspondent. He worked first on the *Daily Telegraph* and *Daily Mail*, moving next to edit the William Hickey column on the *Daily Express* and later the Londoner's Diary for the *Evening Standard*. He has travelled the world covering political and social events, wars, revolutions and disasters. He became an expert on the British royal family the hard way by reporting its activities here and abroad. With the encouragement of Lord Beaverbrook, he broke with the traditional way of writing about living royalty and established the new method of honesty, frankness and candour better suited to the modern age.

Cover photographs:
Princess Anne and Prince Charles, Camera Press;
Prince Andrew and Prince Edward,
Anwar Hussein

THE QUEEN'S CHILDREN

DONALD EDGAR

Hamlyn Paperbacks

To my daughter, Deirdre Francesca

THE QUEEN'S CHILDREN
ISBN 0 600 37428 9

First published in Great Britain 1978
by Arthur Barker Limited
Hamlyn Paperbacks edition 1979
Copyright © Donald Edgar 1978

Hamlyn Paperbacks are published by
The Hamlyn Publishing Group Ltd,
Astronaut House,
Feltham,
Middlesex, England

Made and printed in Great Britain
by Hazell Watson & Viney Ltd, Aylesbury, Bucks

Contents

List of illustrations

Acknowledgements

To Be A King by Dermot Morrah (Hutchinson, 1968) is an account of the early years of Prince Charles and is a valuable source book since much information was supplied by the royal family and Palace officials. *Anne, Portrait of a Princess* by Judith Campbell (Cassell, 1970) also received royal assistance and is consequently highly instructive.

Prince Charles has given two major interviews to the press. The first was with Kenneth Harris and *The Observer* printed it on the ninth and sixteenth of June, 1974. The second was with Stuart Kuttner and this was printed in the *Evening Standard* on the seventh and eighth of January, 1975. Both are extremely valuable. The questions were searching and, clearly, Prince Charles was given the opportunity of carefully considering his replies.

Prince Charles, Princess Anne and, latterly, Prince Andrew, have spoken often to the press, to the radio and on television both in Britain and abroad. Some of their statements were prepared, some 'off the cuff'.

Mr John King, chief librarian of the *Daily Express*, and his staff, were most helpful, making available an immense amount of material.

My gratitude is deep to all who have made possible this study of 'The Queen's Children'.

For the views expressed I am responsible.

Donald Edgar
London, 1979

Introduction

The Queen's children – Charles, Anne, Andrew, Edward – were born ordinary human beings. It is just as well to make that platitudinous remark before recounting all the influences surrounding them since birth which make them quite extraordinary human beings.

As children of the Queen they became from birth important representatives of the British monarchy, which has proved itself a remarkably adaptable institution. Their privileges are immense, separating them from most men and women.

There are children born to rich, sometimes very rich, families. There are children born who will inherit great titles. But to be born a child of the Queen brings not only riches and titles, but a measure of deference and respect and an assured position not only in the United Kingdom and the Commonwealth, but throughout the world.

It is a destiny that is almost impossible for the rest of us to conceive.

This is a hard world for most men and women: a struggle for work, food and housing; only for some an opportunity of a first-class education; uncertainties in business and employment; in sickness, the worry whether the best care will be available. For the children of the Queen these difficulties do not exist. It is the absence of these normal cares that make of the royal children, as they grow up, quite extraordinary human beings.

In the past when monarchies were customary and democratic practices more restricted, such royal privileges were accepted as part of the natural order, scarcely questioned. Now they have an element of absurdity about them.

Can they be justified?

The answer is yes, if the services given back to the nation are of such a special quality that they warrant the privileges.

The Queen's life has shown she is aware of this. In 1977 the nation and the Commonwealth showed their gratitude for her life-time of service.

But such a life demands a self-discipline, a dedication that is rare in anyone, and much more difficult when surrounded by all the opportunities of self-indulgence.

The task of the Queen has not been easy, but she has a character that has matched the task.

Her children certainly face as great a task and, perhaps, thanks to her ground-work in the Commonwealth, even greater opportunities.

Will they be worthy?

It is a daunting question to ask in 1979 when Prince Charles, heir to the throne, is thirty-one, Princess Anne, twenty-nine, Prince Andrew, nineteen and Prince Edward, fifteen.

The Queen and Prince Philip, together with their able advisers, appreciated that their children would grow up in a world increasingly sceptical of hereditary privilege. They knew that the challenges to prove that the monarchy was a valid institution would be constant. The children, especially Charles, heir to the throne, would need a much broader education than that which had been considered adequate in the past for the royal family. Almost from the first there was a general acceptance of the fact that the Queen's children would go away to school. This was acknowledged not only in Buckingham Palace, but by the nation as a whole. Even in the most conservative circles, it seemed to be taken for granted that Charles and, later, the other children would have to learn to rub shoulders from an early age with the outside world, even if they were carefully selected shoulders.

Prince Philip's background was a help. As a young exiled Prince of the Greek royal family he had enjoyed – and really enjoyed – a varied education. A young children's school at St Cloud outside Paris; Cheam preparatory school in England; Hahn's school at Salem in Germany, later transferred to Gordonstoun in Scotland; then the Royal Naval College at Dartmouth to train as a professional naval officer.

For him, the prospect of his children, especially the boys, having a similar education, presented no problems. He was also a very forward-looking, progressive man who welcomed the need for change.

The Queen and her sister, Princess Margaret, had been

educated privately. Both had appreciated its limitations. The restricted life she had led made the Queen painfully shy when after the war she found herself launched on a public career as heir to the throne. Her early marriage to Prince Philip, ebullient, charming and full of loving care, was of inestimable importance to her. In those early days of her career he taught her how to face the world. The consciousness of the failings of her own education made her welcome plans for an education of her children which would equip them for their duties.

The education that has been given them is described in the following pages. It is also possible to recount what they thought of it in their own words in the cases of Charles, Anne and, latterly, Andrew. Edward at fifteen is rightly allowed to keep his thoughts private for a few years.

It is not only their education that the Queen's children have commented on. As they have grown up the Queen has allowed them to express themselves in the press, on radio and television with a freedom unthought of in the past.

Guidance is provided by the efficient public relations advisers at Buckingham Palace, some form of censorship is exercised by the Queen and Prince Philip, but it is astonishing how candid and frank Charles, Anne and Andrew have been, and are, in giving their views to the media on just about every subject under the sun.

There is almost nothing barred. They talk about their parents, the monarchy, sport, literature, love, marriage, clothes, music, theatre . . . they talk with an apparent lack of inhibition just about anything.

This, in itself, makes a fascinating story. It is a story told by themselves.

But as the story unfolds certain questions arise.

Why were all three sons sent to Gordonstoun? Prince Philip went there, but it is a school outside the usual British educational pattern.

How strong is the royal family's connection with their German relatives?

Is Lord Mountbatten an *éminence grise*?

Did Charles's love life get out of hand? When will he

marry? What choice has he for a bride? Has he been thinking of a girl who is Roman Catholic?

Is there an inner significance to his obsession with George III?

Will he continue to brave criticism of his increasing outspokenness on what he considers must be done to put Britain right?

Will Princess Anne carry on with her public duties much longer?

Will Prince Andrew, able, tough and individualistic, settle down in the navy?

Will Prince Edward be given the opportunity to break away from a traditional service career?

One of the Queen's greatest achievements has been to preserve and enhance the position of the British monarch as Head of the Commonwealth. Can her sons carry forward the development and act as links in the new countries of the Commonwealth, giving an example of a working system of multi-racialism?

It is one matter to pose questions, another to answer them satisfactorily. But some tentative answers seem to arise naturally from the story of—the Queen's children.

I

The Unhappy Schoolboy

Prince Charles was born on Sunday evening, 14 November 1948, at Buckingham Palace. His mother, Princess Elizabeth, aged twenty-two, was heir to the throne of her father, King George VI. His father, Prince Philip, of the Greek royal family, by origin Danish-German, was twenty-seven. They had been married in Westminster Abbey on 20 November the previous year. It had been a love match as well as a suitable marriage. Princess Elizabeth, attractive and shy, had already an assured place in the hearts of the nation. Prince Philip, handsome and forthright, educated in Britain and a wartime officer in the Royal Navy, had easily won his own popularity.

Charles came a little late into the world for he had been expected in October. At the time of the birth Prince Philip was playing squash in the Palace court to relieve the tension. When he had seen his wife and son he brought in her parents, the King and Queen. The Dowager Queen Mary, aged eighty, drove from nearby Marlborough House to see her first great-grandchild.

There was champagne for the family, the doctors and the Palace officials. It was a time for contented satisfaction. Elsewhere the efficient machinery for telling the world that the heir to the British throne had been safely delivered of a son went into action.

From the private post office in the Palace piles of telegrams were sent to the governors-general of the dominions and colonies (still numerous at that time), to ambassadors, officials, relatives and friends. The armed forces were alerted so that throughout the world the ceremonial 21-gun salutes would be fired on land and sea. The BBC gave out news bulletins at home and abroad. In Fleet Street the newspapers set the largest types for the headlines. On the next morning flags would be flown officially from all public buildings and spontaneously from many others.

It was a world event. By his birth Charles would be entitled to titles, privileges, honours, wealth. In return he would always be a public, not a private person.

He was baptized on 15 December in the Music Room at the Palace by the Archbishop of Canterbury with water from the River Jordan. The godparents were the King and Queen, Princess Margaret, King Haakon of Norway, the Hon. David Bowes-Lyon, brother of the Queen, and three of Prince Philip's relations – his grandmother, the Dowager Marchioness of Milford Haven, his uncle, Prince George of Greece, and his cousin Lady Brabourne, daughter of Lord Mountbatten.

The names he was given were Charles Philip Arthur George. The first name, Charles, by which he would be known both as Prince, and in the fullness of time, as King, occasioned some surprise. It was a Stuart name held by Kings Charles I and II in the seventeenth century. Since the present royal family came over from Hanover early in the eighteenth century it had had little reason to remember the Stuarts with gratitude, although descended from them on the female side. For in 1715 and 1745 their throne had been endangered in Britain by armed rebellions in favour of a Stuart restoration.

The new Prince Charles was put in the hands of an experienced nanny, Helen Lightbody, who had already looked after the two sons of the Duke and Duchess of Gloucester, Prince William and Prince Richard.

In July the next year, 1949, Princess Elizabeth and Prince Philip moved to Clarence House, a royal mansion near the Palace, which had been extensively refurbished. Princess Anne was born there on Tuesday 15 August 1950. She, too, was greeted with flags flying, gun salutes and messages of congratulation.

She was also baptized in the Music Room at Buckingham Palace. This time the Archbishop of York officiated. She was

given the names Anne Elizabeth Alice Louise and it was remarked that Anne too was a Stuart name. Her sponsors were
the Queen, Princess Andrew of Greece (Prince Philip's
mother), his sister, Princess Margarita of Hohenlohe-
Langenburg, Lord Mountbatten and the Hon. Andrew Elphin-
stone, a relative of the Queen.

Princess Anne joined her brother in the nursery and the
nanny acquired an assistant. It was a period of comparative
anonymity for the children, broken by occasional recognition as
they were pushed in their prams through St James's Park with
an accompanying detective. They followed their parents and
grandparents to the royal houses, Windsor, Sandringham and
Balmoral.

Their mother had an increasing share of public duties.
Prince Philip was serving as a naval officer in the Mediterranean Fleet, based on Malta, then still an important naval
centre for the British. In December 1950 Princess Elizabeth
flew there to spend ten weeks with her husband without the
children, who spent much of the time with the King and Queen
at Sandringham. The King, whose health was not good, found
much comfort in the company of his grandchildren, especially
Charles.

From an early age Charles and Anne were accustomed to the
absences of their parents. What they did not have, they could
not miss, but it meant the nanny was in these early years the
dominating influence.

In 1951 Princess Elizabeth and Prince Philip went to Canada
for their most important Commonwealth tour so far. They returned in the autumn and found the King recovering reasonably well from the serious operation he had recently undergone.
The family spent Christmas at Sandringham as usual and on
31 January Princess Elizabeth and Prince Philip set off by air
on an extended Commonwealth tour, beginning in Africa. The
King looked tired and ill as he waved them good-bye. It was
the last time his daughter was to see him alive. He died in his
sleep on 6 February when she and Prince Philip were in Kenya.

The mother of Charles and Anne was Queen. She was
twenty-five. Charles, who had been three the previous Novem-

ber, was heir to the throne. As eldest son of the sovereign he became Duke of Cornwall and beneficiary of its great revenues. The Dukedom, the first in English history, was created in 1337 by Edward III for his eldest son, Edward, then aged six, and later famed as the warrior Black Prince.

The move to Buckingham Palace following the Queen's accession did not mean much more to Charles and Anne than a change of nurseries. Charles was a quiet, serious child who rarely gave trouble, but Anne, full of energy, was a handful to the staff. At the end of 1952 on his fourth birthday Charles had his biggest party to date. Fourteen children were invited and the band of the Grenadier Guards played in the forecourt his favourite tune, 'The Teddy Bears' Picnic'.

The coronation of the Queen took place on 2 June 1953, and the preparations created a stir in the Palace which reached the nursery. Anne had a dressing-up game and decked herself out as regally as she could. When she heard that Charles, but not herself, would be going to the Abbey to see some of the ceremony, there was a scene. She recalled later, 'there was the usual sisterly fury because my brother went, but I was not allowed to go. I had an argument about it.'

Charles was dressed in a white silk suit and taken by car with his nanny to a side door of the Abbey and put into the royal box between the Queen Mother and Princess Margaret. He can scarcely remember a thing about the scene of splendour now that he is grown up. He was bemused when he saw his mother being anointed with holy oil by the Archbishop and asked so many questions that he was soon led away and driven back to the Palace. Later in the day, however, both he and Anne went out to the Palace balcony with their parents, still arrayed in their coronation pomp, and heard the shouts and cheers of the great crowd.

In November the Queen and Prince Philip were setting off on a six-month tour of the Commonwealth which was to set the seal on the coronation celebrations. As Charles would be five in the same month a governess, Katherine Peebles, was appointed to start his education in a class-room set up in the

Palace. Miss Peebles had already been governess to Prince Michael of Kent.

While the Queen and Prince Philip were away, the Queen Mother and Princess Margaret spent as much time as they could with the children. Anne was finding her feet and her seat. Dolls, dolls' prams and houses, had little appeal. She took over Charles's toy wooden trap with its pony and pedalled vigorously up and down the corridors. There were large gardens and grounds to play in at Buckingham Palace, Windsor, Sandringham and Balmoral. Charles had a tricycle and there were excursions to Richmond Park and Hampstead Heath. Both children were put in the saddle, almost as soon as they could walk, first on a Shetland pony, then on a Welsh mountain pony. They had two corgis, a hamster and two South American love-birds. Miss Vacani, the famous dancing teacher, came to give lessons and a few other children of the court were invited to join in.

In many ways their life was that of other children of the rich. But there were differences, even if Charles and Anne were unaware of them. There were sentries at the gates in scarlet tunics and bearskins. There were waves from groups of sightseers when they passed in one of the royal cars, and they were taught to wave back. When they travelled to Balmoral, they went in the royal train. There was a special nursery coach, air-conditioned and sound-proof, with a bedroom for each, a sitting-room and a bathroom. How special their lives were neither Charles nor Anne could realize. This style was the only one they knew.

In April 1954, there was a break in the routine. The new royal yacht, *Britannia*, was travelling to Tobruk to pick up the Queen and Prince Philip at the end of their world tour. Charles and Anne sailed in the yacht to meet them. They stopped at Malta *en route*, where their father's uncle, Lord Mountbatten, was stationed as Commander-in-Chief of the Mediterranean Fleet. He and his wife, Edwina, showed them round the war-scarred island and the Grand Harbour, still at that time a busy anchorage for the pale-grey British warships. They had a joyful reunion with their parents at Tobruk and on the return journey visited Gibraltar and saw the Barbary apes which, so the myth runs, will be on the Rock as long as the British Empire exists. They seem to be thriving in the new atmosphere of the Commonwealth.

Back home routine was resumed. The Queen and Prince Philip saw their children most mornings at nine o'clock for half an hour. They spent more time with them during the weekends at Windsor and during the autumn and winter holidays at Balmoral and Sandringham.

Anne was happy enough when she was doing what she wanted, but lost her temper when she was thwarted. Nanny knew how to deal with tantrums. Charles got on with his lessons, but was gradually given a few more treats.

He went to the Tower of London, saw the Beefeaters in their Tudor uniform and listened to the stories of his ancestors' deeds and misdeeds. He watched from a balcony as his mother took the salute at the Trooping the Colour ceremony by the Guards on Horse Guards Parade which marks her official birthday. He watched from a gallery the annual service of the Knights of the Garter at St George's, Windsor.

Gradually, he was being indoctrinated into the world that would one day be his.

The rhythm of the children's lives went on gently. In the autumn of 1955, Anne, who had had her fifth birthday in August, started classes in the Palace and was later joined by two girls of around her own age – Caroline Hamilton, eldest granddaughter of the Dean of Windsor, and Susan Babington-Smith.

In the following year arrangements were made for Charles to spend two terms as a day-boy at a school in Knightsbridge. He was a somewhat dreamy, remote boy and it was hoped this would break him into the routine and challenge of being with other boys which it had been decided he would have to face.

The school was Hill House in Hans Place, which lies between Kensington and Chelsea. It was run by Colonel Townend, a former Oxford blue at soccer and a champion skier. There were about a hundred pupils drawn from the professional classes.

Colonel Townend and his staff did their best to make it a happy time for a boy who did not like being at school. Soon after starting in November 1956 he was away for three weeks with tonsilitis. In the second term he had a recurrence of the trouble and his tonsils were taken out. He went down to some friends of the Queen in Norfolk to recover.

However, he became used to being with other boys in class and on the playing-field, and to wearing a school uniform. In class his reading, writing and general knowledge were good. His arithmetic was bad. At sport he tried, but had no natural aptitude, except in swimming, thanks to early training by his father in the Palace swimming pool.

After Hill House he went sailing with his father in August 1957 at Cowes and realized that though he liked the sea, he suffered from seasickness. It has plagued him since. Then it was up to Balmoral with the family. He knew that in September he would be going away as a boarder to Cheam School where his father had been before him. He did not like the prospect. As the day grew nearer he actively detested it.

Cheam was a school of good repute, much favoured by parents who wanted their sons to go into the navy. They turned out products that the Royal Naval College at Dartmouth liked. Certainly it was a Mountbatten navy school. Apart from Prince Philip, his cousin the Marquess of Milford Haven went there before going to Dartmouth.

The school had been at Cheam in Surrey for a couple of centuries, but in the nineteen thirties had moved to Headley, near Newbury in Berkshire. They took around a hundred pupils and had an excellent staff with joint headmasters, Mr Peter Beck and Mr Mark Wheeler. There were seventy acres of playing fields, gardens and woodlands.

David Munir, a mathematics master, had been asked to keep an eye on Charles and remembers him on the first day standing alone, very miserable and 'notably in need of a haircut'. Charles got over the worst of these initial difficulties, but he remembers his early days at Cheam as the time he suffered most from being who he was. The boys fought shy of making an approach to the heir of the throne. That was to be expected. They did not want to be accused of fawning.

He slept in a dormitory, made his own bed, cleaned his shoes and took his turn waiting at table. He wore a grey suit with short trousers. Outside, a blue cap and a blazer.

His first term was nearly his last. The press, British and foreign, pursued news about Charles at his boarding school with relentless energy. Many stories were published, some true, some false. The press was willing to pay for information and by the end of term, masters, boys and staff generally were suffering from mutual suspicion which made life a misery for all. The trouble was that there was no machinery for dealing with press enquiries. They were met with a blank wall.

The man who solved the problem was Mr (later Sir) Edward Pickering, then editor of the *Daily Express*. He suggested to Commander (later Sir) Richard Colville, the Queen's press secretary, that there should be a meeting between Fleet Street editors and the Cheam authorities and a sensible solution found. The meeting was held. The difficulties were ironed out, reasonable enquiries were in future dealt with in a constructive manner and the rest of Charles's days at Cheam passed without great trouble from the press.

Charles was at Cheam from the autumn of 1957 to the spring of 1962, four and a half years. For most of the time life was a misery for him there. Everyone knew it – his parents, the masters and the pupils. It was especially hard on the staff for they had done their best.

He had not done badly at his books. He had tried his best on the playing fields. He had made a few friends. But his heart was not in it.

The Queen inadvertently struck a blow at his attempts to integrate himself at the school before his first year there was finished. In July 1958, she decided, after consulting her advisers and the Prime Minister, to create her son Prince of Wales. She was to speak at the closing of the Empire and Commonwealth Games at Cardiff and would be sure of a great crowd and the presence of the world press. It was a splendid public relations opportunity.

Charles and his headmaster, Peter Beck, were warned in advance. A small gathering of boys was arranged to watch the ceremony on television in Beck's study with Charles. As it happened, the Queen developed sinusitis and her message was taped and introduced by Prince Philip.

Charles sat in the study and heard his mother's voice.

I want to take this opportunity of speaking to all Welsh people, not only in this arena, but wherever they may be. The British Empire and Commonwealth Games in the capital, together with all the activities of the Festival of Wales, have made a memorable year for the Principality. I have, therefore, decided to mark it further by an act which will, I hope, give as much pleasure to all Welshmen as it does to me. I intend to create my son Prince of Wales today. When he is grown up I will present him to you at Caernarvon.

The date was Saturday 26 July 1958. Charles would be ten in November.

Back at Cheam the boys surrounding Charles clapped and cheered. He was overcome with embarrassment. He has never forgotten the moment. He wished, as they say, he could have sunk into the ground.

As Prince of Wales Charles became automatically a Knight of the Garter, the oldest order of chivalry. He also became Earl of Chester. His titles and style now ran: His Royal Highness Prince Charles Philip Arthur George, Prince of Wales and Earl of Chester, Duke of Cornwall, Duke of Rothesay, Earl of Carrick, Lord of the Isles and Baron of Renfrew, Prince and Great Steward of Scotland, Knight Companion of the Most Noble Order of the Garter.

While Charles was passing these years at Cheam, unhappy and mediocre of achievement, Anne was having her lessons at the Palace and was also unhappy and not shining at her work. The classical name for her was a tomboy. She was angry that Charles had been allowed to go to school and not herself. Her parents had decided that she would not leave the Palace until she was thirteen, in 1963, and would then go as a boarder. There were a number of excellent day schools in London where

Anne could early have learned to come to terms with other girls. She wanted this opportunity and was probably right. Instead, taking lessons with a few girls drawn from the court circle, she grew surly and allowed her natural intelligence to lie fallow.

She needed activity outside the narrow court circle. She was active, friendly and pleasant with the other girls who formed part of the Brownie Pack – junior Girl Guides – which was specially got together in May 1959 to learn and play in the gardens of Buckingham Palace. But the meetings were not frequent.

In 1960, nearly ten years after the birth of Anne, the Queen had her third child. He was a son, born on 19 February, and was christened Andrew Albert Christian Edward.

Anne was twice a bridesmaid this year at family weddings. The first was in January when Lady Pamela Mountbatten, the younger daughter of Lord Mountbatten, married Mr David Hicks, an interior decorator, at Romsey Abbey. The second was on 6 May when she was chief bridesmaid when her aunt, Princess Margaret, married Mr Antony Armstrong-Jones, a photographer (created Earl of Snowdon), in Westminster Abbey. Anne looked very well in a long gown and with her hair arranged high on her head.

As the Brownie Pack had been a success, in May 1961 Anne became a Girl Guide in the 1st Buckingham Palace Company. The girls were not only from the court families, but represented a fair cross-section of the community in Central London. They met once a week in the summerhouse in the Palace gardens. When the Queen was free she invited one or two of the girls in turn to take tea with her and Anne. For Anne it was a welcome break. She showed another side of her nature – co-operative and helpful. She enjoyed taking part in the play they put on each Christmas – one year a nativity play, the next a panto-mime.

The new Prince, Andrew, had his first public showing in 1961. After Trooping the Colour on her official birthday, 10 June, the Queen usually appears in her Guards uniform on the balcony of Buckingham Palace to acknowledge the cheers of the crowds. This year she was carrying Andrew in her arms.

As Charles and Anne were growing up, they were given all the appropriate initiations. Charles shot his first grouse and was blooded after a kill by foxhounds. He learned ice-skating at Richmond from an expert. Anne had Miss Vacani for dancing and an exceptionally able young Frenchwoman to help her French accent. She also went sailing with her father and discovered that, like her brother, she suffered badly from sea-sickness.

In February 1962, Charles went down with appendicitis at Cheam. He was operated on at Great Ormond Street Hospital and then went to Windsor to convalesce. It marked just about the end of his years at Cheam for he was not going back for the summer term.

He was to go to Gordonstoun on 1 May.

Prince Philip had been a success at Cheam and then Gordonstoun. Charles had not been a success at Cheam. He had disliked his years there. But, inexorably, he was to go to Gordonstoun.

This summer Anne was twelve, Charles thirteen and a half. It could be said that they were both problem children, or, as they say, children with problems. It could not be said that the educational programme organized so far by the Queen and Prince Philip – especially by Prince Philip in the case of Charles – was proving even moderately successful.

2

Why Gordonstoun?

Gordonstoun has achieved a remarkable place in British education. The three Princes, Charles, Andrew and Edward, have all attended this school which was founded in Germany in the nineteen twenties. They have been sent there in preference to the many historic and prestigious public schools. It was a break in tradition that the royal children should be sent away to school. It is quite extraordinary that all three boys should have been sent to Gordonstoun.

Their father, Prince Philip, attended the school at its original home at Salem in Germany and then later, on its transfer to Scotland, at Gordonstoun. He profoundly respects the educational philosophy of the founder, Kurt Hahn, and believes the school is superior to any other in Britain.

The proof of the pudding will be in the eating. The careers of Charles, Andrew and Edward will inevitably be judged to a certain extent in terms of the Gordonstoun background. Certainly the choice of school has been a blow to the British public schools, especially to Eton with its historic role as educator of the sons of the noble, the rich and the influential.

Kurt Hahn was born into one of those rich Jewish families of the higher bourgeoisie whose wealth and culture enabled them to play a considerable part in the German Empire which had been proclaimed at Versailles in 1871 after the defeat of France. Such Jews were sometimes known as *Junkerjuden*, or Jews of the aristocracy. It is one of the ironies of history that in Imperial Germany the Jews felt themselves more integrated than in most other countries. They were extremely patriotic, served the state with complete loyalty and contributed with their intellectual and commercial talents to the rising German ambitions.

Hahn was a brilliant young man and after his university days came to Oxford as a Rhodes Scholar before the First World War. He made influential friends, went on long walking expeditions, as was the habit of young scholars in those days, and studied England and its institutions. Particularly he studied the way the English educated their élite in the public schools and universities. He admired the easy freedom of Eton which concealed an instinctive acceptance of unchallengeable traditions. In the new unified Germany, an amalgam of widely different states, the now dominant Prussian spirit was being drilled with relentless efficiency into the youth. Hahn was able to compare the British and German systems, having at the back of his mind the educational precepts of Plato's *Republic* which was to him, as to many scholar-politicians of the time in Germany and Britain, almost a bible of revealed knowledge.

When the First World War broke out Hahn was employed by the German Foreign Office as an expert on England. One of his duties was to advise on the state of mind of the enemy and he studied the British press which reached Berlin through neutral countries. Towards the end of the war he attracted the attention of Prince Max of Baden, the last Imperial Chancellor, and became his secretary. When Germany collapsed in 1918, riven by revolution, many of the German ruling families retired to their estates. They had time to reflect on the reasons for the defeat of Germany. Now Hahn came into his own. He persuaded Prince Max that the education of the German élite had been at fault. By comparison the British system had proved superior. Their young leaders had shown an unbreakable spirit in the face of disaster.

He asked for help to set up a school which would embody a new system, drawing both from British and German experience and influenced by the educational ideals of Plato. Hahn was fortunate. He had a patron who was willing and able to help. Prince Max owned a vast former monastery at Salem in South Germany in the beautiful country that slopes down to

Lake Constance. There he offered facilities to set up the new school.

The early pupils were drawn from the German princely and aristocratic families with some sons of the great industrial and commercial dynasties. As its fame spread, some of the rich German families abroad, especially in South America, sent their sons to Salem. Prince Philip, after his years at Cheam, was sent there by his relatives, the Mountbattens.

There was a profound earnestness about the Hahn system which was more German than British. The emphasis on the building of character and physical health was so strong that it seems almost a caricature of the British public school system. Prince Charles said years later: 'Gordonstoun developed my will-power and self-control, helped me to discipline myself, and I think that discipline, not in the sense of making you bath in cold water, but in the Latin sense – giving shape and form and tidiness to your life – is the most important thing your education can do.'

When Hitler came to power in 1933, Hahn soon came into conflict with the Nazis. He was of a Jewish family and he was educating a privileged group of boys from the noble families for which Hitler had little time. The Nazis wished to train their own Aryan élite through the SS with very different concepts of life.

Hahn was imprisoned for a short time, but powerful influences in Britain were working for him and he was allowed to come to this country. Leading academics including the headmaster of Eton, the Archbishop of Canterbury and John Buchan (later Lord Tweedsmuir), author and proconsul, knew of his work at Salem, approved of it, and helped him to set up school at Gordonstoun in the remote county of Morayshire.

Hahn's courage in Germany was admirable. Just before Hitler came to power a particularly brutal murder had been committed by the Nazis. Hahn wrote to the old boys of Salem, 'It is a question now in Germany of its Christian morality, its reputation, its soldierly honour: Salem cannot remain neutral. I call on all members of the Salem Association who are active in the SA or the SS to terminate their allegiance either to Hitler or to Salem.' Sir Robert Birley, headmaster of Eton from 1949 to 1963, recounting this adds that Hahn made his stand at a time when all the great German universities, Heidelberg, Jena, Goettingen, remained silent.

Donald McLachlan, distinguished in education and journalism, who knew Hahn well, wrote that his diagnosis remained in essence unchanged over forty years:

> The young today are surrounded by tempting declines – declines which affect the adult world – the decline of fitness, due to modern methods of moving about; decline of memory and imagination, due to the confused restlessness of modern life; decline of skill and care, due to the weakened tradition of craftsmanship; decline of self-discipline, due to stimulants and tranquillisers. Worst of all, the decline in compassion, due to the unseemly haste with which life is conducted.

Hahn asked his audiences: 'What is it that is done to our children that their puberty should deform them? They have the joy of movement; they have an enterprising curiosity; they are ready for sensible self-denial; they dream ahead, and they have a faithful memory, and above all, great compassion.'

He saw his mission as an attempt to preserve those qualities.

Life at Gordonstoun was austere, but perhaps its austerity has been exaggerated. Life at most British public schools is not exactly a bed of roses. Any reservation one may have about Hahn's philosophy is perhaps that he was inspired by Plato. For the Greek philosopher despised the democracy of his native Athens which had been defeated by the military machine of Sparta. Plato admired Sparta and his educational system is designed to create an aristocracy consciously fashioned to rule. Whereas the British public school education owes more than a little to the ideals of the Renaissance expressed in Castiglione's *The Book of the Courtier*. The aim was to produce a gentleman rather than a ruler – a Philip Sidney, poet, scholar and warrior, rather than a Bismarck.

After the 1939–45 war the Gordonstoun system became more popular. Hahn's noble resistance to the Nazis was one factor. Another, undoubtedly, was Prince Philip, who by marrying Princess Elizabeth, heir to the British crown, had become a person of great influence. He was the most notable Gordonstoun product to date and wrote and spoke of Hahn's aim to encourage boys to develop as responsible individuals, 'strong enough in mind and character to reject the standards of the mob and to resist the temptation to run with the herd'. It is fair to point out that the 'mob' and 'herd' to repeat Prince Philip's emotive words, may be a democratic majority which has other ideals than those of Gordonstoun.

Philip's Duke of Edinburgh Award Scheme was inspired by Gordonstoun thinking. So were the Outward Bound courses, designed to challenge the urban young with the mountains and the sea. In Greece a small-scale Gordonstoun was founded at Anafryta under the patronage of Queen Frederika, a close relative of Prince Philip. Her son, Prince Constantine (later King of Greece and now in exile), was educated there.

Other schools were founded in Britain, Germany, Nigeria and the United States. Even more schools throughout the world established links with Gordonstoun through exchanges of boys and teachers. The first international Atlantic College was started at St Donat's Castle in Wales for sixth-formers from various countries to inculcate Gordonstoun ideals before they went on to university or professional training. Lord Mountbatten became chairman of the College, renamed the United World College of the Atlantic.

Prince Charles has said that he was not made to follow in his father's footsteps to Gordonstoun. He recounts that at the time his years at Cheam were coming to an end, Prince Philip told him the pros and cons of all the possible schools and advised him what he thought was best. 'Then he left me to decide', says Charles. 'I freely subjected myself to what he thought was best because I had come to see how wise he was. By the time I had to be educated I had perfect confidence in my father's judgment.' At the time Charles was thirteen.

The Queen had been told much about Gordonstoun over the years by Prince Philip. In October 1961, she went to see the school and came away convinced by her husband and the headmaster that such criticism as had been levelled against the system (including some by ex-pupils) was unfair and agreed that Charles should go there. Her decision met criticism in her own family and among her advisers.

It was felt that the Queen in her admiration for her husband had been reluctant to thwart his wishes. But other considerations, more deep-seated, may well have played a part in the Queen's decision. The Queen, as she often says, is very family-minded and her family is overwhelmingly German. Many of her German relatives were kings and queens, princes and princesses of European monarchies that have now been swept away. But the family links remain. These relatives naturally look up to the Queen, monarch of a prestigious country and head of a world-wide Commonwealth. She is conscious of the fact.

For many years after 1945 feeling against the Germans ran high in Britain and the Queen realized it would be unwise to entertain her German relatives here with too much publicity. She did invite them over privately, however, especially to Balmoral in the summer and autumn. It is an estate relatively secluded from the attentions of the press.

Prince Philip went over to Germany with increasing frequency to see his three surviving sisters and their families. They are Margarita, wife of Gottfried von Hohenlohe-Langenburg, grandson of Alfred, Duke of Edinburgh; Theodora, wife of Berthold, Margrave of Baden; and Sophie, married to Prince George William of Hanover, brother of Queen Frederika of Greece and first headmaster of Salem, the original Gordonstoun, when it was re-opened after the war. Philip's sisters have seventeen children between them, cousins of the British royal children.

When the Queen came to consider where Charles should go to school, Eton would have been in many ways a natural choice. It is an institution which is part of the fabric of British life. Gordonstoun, apart from the fact that Prince Philip went there, was a partially German creation, whose original patrons had been largely her German relatives. An education at Gordonstoun was an education in Britain, but it was not an education, as at Eton, essentially and exclusively British. It did, however, provide a link with the Queen's European relatives and their approach to life.

In the Easter holidays of 1962, just before Charles started at Gordonstoun, Prince Philip took him to Germany to see some of his relatives. They visited his sister Sophie and her husband Prince George. One of their sons, Prince Guelf (there is no name more evocative to the royal family for it is the name of their founder) had already been to Balmoral. He was two years older than Charles and would be at Gordonstoun with him. Prince Philip then took Charles to see his sister Theodora and her family. This was Charles's first visit to Germany. He was given the chance of meeting agreeable relatives and getting some feel for the roots of his family.

These princes and dukes may have lost their authority as rulers, but, by and large, they are still impressive. They have their estates and castles. On grand family occasions, such as a marriage, they put on a fine show and, as likely as not, there at the head of the visiting dignitaries will be Lord Mountbatten, wearing a splendid uniform and one of his many sashes. He occupies a formidable position. He is not only of the House of Hesse, but a descendant of Queen Victoria and uncle of Prince Philip, with a service career of immense distinction behind him. He is for the German relatives of the great family a symbol of prestige and achievement.

Charles is well aware of Lord Mountbatten's position. 'He is, I think, the centre of the family', he has said. 'The last person of his generation that knew everybody. He was brought up to think very strongly that the family was an important concept, which I do feel very deeply too. Certainly Lord Mountbatten has had an influence on my life and I admire him, I think, almost more than anybody else. He's a very great person.'

On 1 May 1962, Prince Philip delivered Prince Charles to the headmaster of Gordonstoun, Mr F. R. G. Chew. Charles already had relatives there apart from Prince Guelf, for Norton Knatchbull, Lord Mountbatten's grandson, was also a pupil. He was the eldest of the sons of Lord Brabourne, who was married to Lady Patricia Mountbatten, and all five of them were destined for Gordonstoun.

But all the careful preparations for Charles were fruitless. If the first days at Cheam had been bad enough, Gordonstoun was worse.

3
High Jinks for Anne

Anne went to her first Guide camp in June 1962. It was in Sussex and everyone – even those in charge – seemed to have a good time. She was at her best, full of fun and energy, taking her turn with all the chores whether it was cleaning the latrines or handling crates of food and milk.

In July she went to France with Mrs Untermeyer who had taught French to the Queen and Princess Margaret. They stayed with the Marquis de St Genys in the Loire Valley, France's 'royal valley' because of the numerous royal *châteaux*, and efforts were made to improve Anne's accent.

She was twelve in August. She was passing through the period of puberty and with her, as with most other girls, it brought problems. With Anne they expressed themselves in an increasing resentment about life in general and a sub-conscious revolt against the fact that she was a girl and would become a woman. The attitude is not unusual, especially amongst the English. Anne was bossy, moody, brusque. Her education, still confined to the Palace, restricted her, while her brother Charles was launched into Gordonstoun – a challenge which Anne was sure she would have taken in her stride.

About this time her parents gave her a pony called High Jinks and this, in the opinion of Judith Campbell, who has written about Anne and her horses in several perceptive books with the help and approval of the royal family, 'was a turning-point in Princess Anne's riding career, and, in some ways, in her life apart from the sport.'

Anne was always good on her early ponies which she shared with Charles – William from Ireland and the Welsh mare,

Greensleeves. The two children went to the Smiths' famous riding school at Holyport, near Windsor. Miss Sybil Smith was carrying on the skills which her father had employed on so many pupils, including the Queen when she was a girl. Anne showed a lot of courage and had a natural sense of horsemanship.

There was everything to encourage Anne – a mother devoted to horses, a father whom she used to watch playing polo on Smith's Lawn at Windsor. Her own enthusiasm, she found, made her more interesting to those around her and attracted that extra degree of attention which was so important to her.

Anne was ten when the Crown Equerry, Colonel (later Sir) John Miller, acquired the cream-coloured pony, Bandit, for Charles and Anne. It was she who made most use of him. At Windsor a small cross-country course was set up for her in the Home Park and other girls were invited to take part in competitions organized by Miller. She and Charles competed in a few gymkhanas as members of the Garth Pony Club. But it was mainly for Anne that Bandit was sent up to Norfolk and Scotland when the family stayed there.

With the arrival of High Jinks, her own pony, life began to change for Anne. It was not only a symbol of freedom from people. As her skill increased, she began to have ambitions not just to ride, but to ride in the championship class. Music meant little to Anne. She had failed with the piano and the pop music of the radio and disc was more her taste. Words had only meaning for her, no magic. Art, surrounded as she was by one of the great collections, made small impact. But with horses she felt alive and confident.

She would show them all – family, world – that there was something she could do well on her own account and not as Princess Anne. She had the courage and determination, and she had the opportunity. It was up to her.

At Gordonstoun Prince Charles settled down as best he could. Prince Guelf and he teamed up and the routine, as most routines do, became bearable. He had a rough time in a canoeing expedition carried out in the spirit of the school motto, 'Plus est en vous' ('There is more in you'). The crew had to make their way from Hopeman Beach to Findhorn Bay, about twelve miles direct, but twice the distance allowing for tides and currents. The weather worsened and Charles arrived back just about in a state of collapse.

At the end of this first term he flew back home with Prince Guelf and another pupil, Prince Alexander of the exiled royal family of Yugoslavia. Term had ended with a good report and a measure of achievement, but not much of happiness.

After Christmas Charles went for a winter holiday with his German relatives. He flew to Bavaria to join up with Prince Guelf and his parents, Prince George and Princess Sophie of Hanover. Then Charles, Guelf, and a younger brother and sister were driven through snow-covered Bavaria and Switzerland to the village of Tarasp, not far from the fashionable ski-ing resorts of Davos and St Moritz. There another relative, Prince Ludwig of Hesse and his wife, Margarete, had a fine villa, Haus Muntanetz. The plan was to teach Charles the rudiments of ski-ing, but when he went on the slopes with his instructor he was pursued by a large crowd of photographers and tourists. It became an unseemly free-for-all, as could confidently have been predicted. For the Palace press office had fallen down on their job. There was no one to organize a sensible photographic session, no one to issue statements and bring some order into what developed into a squalid affair. There was Princess Margarete wailing, 'Please leave us alone now. Think of your own boys', to a group of relentless photographers who had an event to cover and a living to earn. Finally, Charles took his ski-ing lessons in the grounds of the estate, protected by a hurriedly reinforced patrol of Swiss Police on skis.

On his way home Charles went to see his aunt Theodora of Baden at Salem.

A few months later, in April 1963, it was the turn of Princess Anne to visit Germany. Prince Philip introduced her to aunts, uncles and cousins. It was a compliment to the German relatives; it was pleasant for Prince Philip to present his daughter.

Almost immediately on her return Anne was a bridesmaid

again. Princess Alexandra, the Queen's cousin and daughter of the widowed Duchess of Kent, was married in Westminster Abbey to the Hon. Angus Ogilvy, second son of the Earl of Arlie, who had been Lord Chamberlain to the Queen Mother. It was a very popular marriage. Alexandra was both beautiful and charming. Ogilvy was handsome and had gone off to make a career for himself in the city.

If Charles had any illusions left that he was an ordinary boy to be treated just like any other boy, they were finally destroyed in June. He was on a seamanship course with other Gordonstoun boys in the *Pinta*, one of two fine ketches owned by the school. They were on a week's cruise among the Outer Hebrides and put in at Stornoway on the Isle of Lewis for a meal and a visit to the cinema. Charles's detective left the boys in the lounge of the Crown Hotel while he went to book seats for the film. Charles had by now been recognized in the town by the locals and at this time of the year there were also quite a number of visitors. In the hotel Charles found himself being peered at through the windows and suddenly he felt, 'I can't bear this any more. The only other place was the bar. There I thought it best to have a drink. And being terrified not knowing what to do I said the first drink that came into my mind which happened to be cherry brandy because I'd drunk it before when it was cold out shooting.'

Unfortunately for Charles, the local press had been alerted and a freelance woman journalist was in the bar and saw Charles have his drink. From distant Stornoway the news was flashed to London and built up by the British press into a big story which was then picked up by the world press. The nub of the matter was that Charles, aged fourteen, had broken the law by drinking on licensed premises well under the permitted age. He had also broken the rules of Gordonstoun.

The Palace press office spoke to Charles's detective and thought fit to issue a denial of the story. This made matters worse. The original news story was confirmed. The Palace issued a retraction of its denial, and the press naturally made the most of it.

There were some people who had a moral right to feel in-

dignant – certain strict followers of nonconformist churches
and teetotallers. The climate of opinion in these post-war
years had so far relaxed, however, that the story brought no
more response than a chuckle from most.

Charles was punished at Gordonstoun. The detective, after
a decent lapse of time, was transferred. The magnification of
the story in the media, nationally and internationally, had its
effect on Charles.

For many years the woman journalist was for Charles 'that
dreadful woman'.

Anne went for her second Guide camp at the end of July
1963. It was at Maldon Island and she was once more a good,
cheery member of the company. The big event in her life this
year, however, was going away to school. Her parents had decided on Benenden in Kent. It was an expensive school of
around three hundred pupils from twelve and a half upwards.
Anne was thirteen in the August and started in the September.
The school had an excellent reputation as a quiet, hard-
working and disciplined institution. The headmistress, Miss E.
B. Clarke, and her staff were naturally pleased that the Queen
had chosen their school, but their pleasure was muted by a
fear that the arrival of the Princess would upset their peaceful
rhythm. They remembered the troubles Cheam had had for a
time with photographers and snoopers when Charles was there.

Anne's arrival was formal. The Queen went with her. The
entire school was on parade and the press had been allowed to
attend and take photographs. Anne was introduced to the
teachers. The Queen departed and Anne was on her own,
except for the obligatory detective.

Anne is in some ways an extrovert compared with her
brother Charles, but she still found it difficult at first to settle
down. She had been brought up in a narrow circle and the
noise and chatter of a school grated on her. Being essentially
a tough character, however, she soon came to terms with the
regime. She was never what is called a charming girl. She
could be terse to the point of brusqueness. School was another
fence and it was not going to defeat Anne.

She became a good lacrosse player and her tennis, for which

she had already had excellent Wimbledon coaches, was of a
fair standard. The great joy of the week for Anne was the
riding session at Moat House, a nearby riding school patron-
ized by the school and run by a first-class horsewoman, Mrs
Hatton-Hall, who as Cherry Kendall was a well-known and
successful competitor at Badminton where the Horse Trials
are the premier event of the equestrian year. After Anne's
first term, her pony, High Jinks, was stabled at Moat House
during term-time.

Into riding Anne put all her enthusiasm and intelligence. So
far as her school work was concerned she was naturally bright.
But she took the easy way. She was quite good at English, very
fair at history and geography, but when it came to mathematics she just became obstinate and refused to apply herself.
Another girl would have been pushed harder by the school-
mistress. She got away with it.

On 10 March 1964, the Queen gave birth to her fourth
child, and third son. He was christened Edward Antony
Richard Louis (Antony after the Earl of Snowdon, Richard
after his cousin, the present Duke of Gloucester and Louis
after Prince Louis of Hesse). Both Charles and Anne were
given time off from school to see their mother and their new
brother. The Queen was thirty-eight and it was thought wise
to take life a little more easily for a few weeks. But she was
soon back in form.

Prince Andrew, meanwhile, was developing into an energetic, stubborn child with whom the staff found it difficult to
cope. He was one of those children of whom it is said, 'he's
all right when he gets his own way'.

At Gordonstoun Prince Charles had joined the Combined
Cadet Force, and in the late spring of 1964 he transferred
from the army to the navy section and went to Portsmouth to
do a few weeks with the other boys at HMS *Vernon*, the RN's
shore training centre. He thoroughly enjoyed this and felt
more at home in the navy than in the army. By this time he
was developing an interest in history. He said later: 'I don't
know whether it's me, or being born into what I was, but I *feel*
history. It fascinates me. I'm a romantic at heart, really.' He

also made a start on archaeology. One of the masters got together a group of boys including Charles and they did some cave digging in the area.

In the summer he took his o-levels and the results were about what he had expected. He passed in Latin, French, History, English Language and Literature, but failed in Mathematics and Physics. He was not going to be beaten by his mathematics. He plodded on and finally took the paper successfully eighteen months later.

At the end of term Charles was given permission by his parents to invite a party of Gordonstoun boys to go camping with him for a few days on the Balmoral estate. After two days under canvas Charles started to run a temperature, was found to have pneumonia and taken to a nursing-home at Aberdeen. Thanks to modern drugs, pneumonia is not as serious as it used to be, but his mother flew up to see him. He was up and about in a few weeks and joined his father at Cowes for the yachting.

In September Charles and Anne went to Athens with their father for a great royal social event which was not without political undertones. The young King Constantine of Greece was being married to Princess Anne-Marie of Denmark. Prince Philip, before he renounced the titles on becoming a British subject, was a Prince of both Greece and Denmark.

When Greece finally wrested its independence from Turkey in the nineteenth century the great European powers decided that the new country needed a monarchy, and a suitable candidate was found in the Danish royal family. A complicated relationship was inevitable between the new Greek royal house and its poor, proud, tough people, half-orientalized by centuries of Turkish rule, yet conscious of a past that linked them to the immortal city-states of the classical era. The new Kings from Scandinavia resembled the leaders of the Dorian tribes which had swept down and conquered Greece in pre-classical times. In modern times the Greeks are Levantines, short, swarthy, fierce and hardy on land and sea, both in battle and commerce.

When the Greeks felt they had reason to give affection to

their new royalty they gave it demonstratively. When they decided they did not like their royalty, they turned on them with
ferocity. The Greek royal family, therefore, became accustomed both to rule and exile.

Prince Philip's father had commanded a corps in the Greek-
Turkish war in the early twenties in which the Greeks had
been badly defeated. Prince Andrew, with other high-ranking
officers, was arrested and in danger of execution. It was thanks
to King George V, conscious of his failure to save the lives of
the Russian royal family a few years earlier, that Prince
Andrew was saved and went into exile with the rest of the
Greek royal family. Prince Philip was a baby who had been
sent to the relative safety of Corfu and was picked up there by
a British warship.

On the face of it Prince Philip had no reason to love the
Greeks, but the fact remains that he was born a Prince of
Greece and the Greek royal family is his family. This may
explain why after his marriage to Princess Elizabeth when he
was serving as a naval officer in the Mediterranean he was so
eager to take his wife to Athens in his ship. It was with pride,
too, that he took his two eldest children to Athens in the
autumn of 1964 to play a part in the royal wedding.

This visit, however, was viewed with mixed feelings in
Britain. The Greek monarch is King of the Hellenes, an am-
bitious and provocative title which claims rule over Greeks
wherever and under whatever jurisdiction they happen to live.
During the fifties the Greek Cypriots, led by Archbishop
Makarios and supported by Queen Frederika, launched their
campaign for freedom from their status as a British colony.
The aim was *Enosis*, or union with Greece. The Greek Cypriot
revolution was a long and, at times, bloody affair which at its
height held down thirty thousand British troops. The presence
in Athens of Prince Philip and his children, as well as Princess
Marina of Kent, now raised a question of loyalties. It seemed
that the British royal family was being used to bolster a rickety
Balkan monarchy which had not only shown ingratitude for
vital British help in the struggle against the Communists after
the war, but had aided and applauded the murder of Britons

in Cyprus. Just how precarious was the Greek monarchy was demonstrated a few years later when it was exiled once again.

Be that as it may, the Greek royal wedding was an event of major importance for Charles and Anne, not only because it served to re-emphasize their strong family connection with foreign royalty but also because they each played a vital role in the ceremony. Princess Anne was the senior bridesmaid, while Prince Charles had a more onerous task. The Greeks belong to the Eastern Church, and during the marriage crowns are held over the heads of bride and groom. Ten young men perform the service in rotation. Charles was one of the team and found the task, which employs muscles not normally used, rather exhausting. Frederika, the Queen Mother, had to come to his aid.

The Greek wedding turned out to be something of a royal social gala. Never for many a year had the royal and princely families of Europe had such a get-together. An artificial Ruritanian atmosphere prevailed. The guests were nearly all in exile, or living in republics where their titles had no more than a courtesy value, but for a few days it was as if the last fifty years had not happened. The guest list was a roll-call of the Almanach de Gotha with everyone related and bearing titles that would weigh down ordinary mortals. The dominant note was inevitably German, for the German states had provided either directly, or by marriage, the royal families of Europe.

Both the men and the women looked extremely elegant and most of them wore that air of careless ease that comes to those who spend their lives on beaches and in ski-resorts, with a little hunting in the country and a little shopping in the cities. They may not have known how to preserve their monarchies, but they have certainly known how to survive personally.

There were balls, receptions, swimming parties on the coast – an endless round of festivities given with a lavishness that would have surprised richer countries. The sun shone. The Greeks filled the streets, cheering and waving. The wine flowed. There was music and laughter. It was *opéra bouffe*.

Charles was involved in one disagreeable brush with the international press; it was probable that something like it would happen in that heady atmosphere. A group of young princes and princesses, among them Charles, Anne and Carl Gustav, then the Swedish Crown Prince, were bathing from a raft off a fashionable beach near Athens. Three French photographers evaded the circle of Greek police boats and got close to the raft. There are various versions of what happened then. But two photographers landed in the sea. Charles and his friends hugely enjoyed the proceedings and some of the French press carried indignant reports of their behaviour. Charles, who had seen his father deal brusquely with photographers who interfered with his racing at Cowes, was used to considering them fair game.

Anne went back to Benenden with all the aura of the glamorous royal wedding in Athens. The girls had seen her on television and they had seen her pictures in the papers. For these adolescents who shared her life at school the events marked Anne off from their own lives. Even though they came from relatively privileged families they would never be bridesmaids at a royal wedding and would be unlikely to go dancing and swimming with princes. When Anne was asked about it all, however, she replied brusquely that it had all been just a few days off among her relatives.

At the riding school, she was finding Mrs Hatton-Hall a tough disciplinarian, and because she wanted to shine as a horsewoman, she accepted it. For Anne riding up to now had been largely a matter of going hell-for-leather and hoping for the best. But at Moat House she found herself part of a class spending hours in a covered school circling at walk, trot and canter, with and without stirrups, responding to crisp orders and starting to learn some of the mysteries of looking after and knowing a horse. It was a boring process of training, but Anne stuck it out, partially because some of the other girls were proving as good as, if not better than, she was. Since she wanted to excel, her competitive spirit triumphed.

She not only rode High Jinks, now just Jinks, but other ponies and horses available. By the summer of 1964 she was riding in the Benenden School 'A' Team which won the Combined Training Cup at the Open Day.

After the pleasures of Athens Charles went back to Gordonstoun and soon found himself enmeshed in another press story which embittered him for many years. It also brought an unpleasant atmosphere which soured both the staff and boys.

One of his exercise books was stolen and put up for sale to the press. The fact became known and Scotland Yard was brought in. The book, containing harmless essays such as any schoolboy might have written, was traced to the Mercury Press in St Helens, Lancashire, and seized by the police. Photostat copies had, however, been made and in November the widely-read Hamburg news magazine, *Der Stern*, published translations of the essays. The Palace press office issued a statement regretting that 'the private essay of a schoolboy should have been published in this way'.

Der Stern had also commented that the Prince of Wales had sold the exercise book to another boy for thirty shillings because he was short of pocket-money. The powerful American news magazine, *Time*, often critical of Britain and especially of its traditions, then got to work. It printed a story that Charles, always short of cash, had been in the habit of selling his autograph at Cheam. His lack of funds they said was notorious and they headed the article, 'The Princely Pauper'. *Time*'s investigating team also said that the exercise book had brought in £4000.

Years later in a radio interview with Jack de Manio, Charles said, 'I didn't sell it anyway.' De Manio added, 'You didn't sell it, but somebody else flogged it, I think.' To which Charles replied: 'Well, I think they must have done. Yes, my housemaster, poor man, was accused of selling it for some extraordinary sum in the local pub in Elgin. But he, of course, vehemently denied this. I don't know ... I think somebody must have perhaps have come up from London or anywhere and taken it out of the classroom and then sold it.'

Time was so powerful a magazine, both in the United States and internationally, that Prince Charles's parents decided that something had to be done. An indignant denial was sent to the magazine and was printed. It ran:

There is no truth whatever in the story that Prince Charles has sold his composition book to a classmate. In the first place he is too intelligent and old enough to realize how embarrassing this would turn out to be, and second he is only too conscious of the interest of the press in anything to do with himself and his family. The suggestion that his parents keep him so short of money that he has to find other means to raise it is also a complete invention. Finally, the police would not have attempted to regain the composition book unless they were quite satisfied that it had been obtained illegally.

It was a wretched time for Charles to be the centre of such a story now going round the world. He felt humiliated at the accusations that he was willing to cash in unscrupulously on his position. His parents might shrug it off, because they were experienced in the ways of the world, but he could not. He also knew that it had harmed his relationships at Gordonstoun, relationships which he had painstakingly tried to build up to the best of his ability.

It was no wonder that Charles increasingly wandered off on his own among the hills. He had every reason to wonder whether the daily struggle was justified. He said later to Stuart Kuttner of the London *Evening Standard*:

In a sense one is alone. And the older I get the more alone I become. People may be nervous on meeting me and it takes a bit of time before they are aware that they're not necessarily sucking up or trying to make an impression by talking to me.

A lot of people are frightened I think of what other people would think of them if they came up and talked to me. But there are those people, and I can see them coming a mile off, who are rather 'pushing' and over-enthusiastic and it's usually from some ulterior motive. You know what I mean, they're not the nicest. Unfortunately the nicest people are those who won't come up and make themselves known. I think, 'Good God! What's wrong? Do I smell? Have I changed my shoes?'

I remember when I was much younger, thinking: 'What can be wrong?'

4
The Australian Experiment

After the ritual family Christmas at the end of 1964 Prince Philip took Charles and Anne to Europe again. They went to stay with Prince Franz Josef and his wife, Princess Gina, in the tiny state of Liechtenstein, which has achieved fame as a tax-haven.

It was a ski-ing holiday. For Anne this was her first attempt at a sport which appealed to her. After the disastrous press episode during Charles's first ski-ing holiday in Switzerland, a sensible arrangement was made with the photographers. Charles and Anne were left in peace on the ski slopes in the morning. In the afternoon there was a short photographic session.

Charles, as was to be expected after his recent experiences, had developed a certain antagonism towards the press generally. He knew the photographers must be allowed to take pictures. But he looked as he felt – bloody-minded.

Back at Gordonstoun the pattern of life became somewhat more agreeable for Charles now that O-levels were behind him. He was now a senior boy with his own study. His reading widened and the study programme was more flexible. Music, always an interest, became an intense pleasure. One night he was at the Festival Hall and decided to have a go at the cello. Jacqueline du Pré was playing with her husband, Daniel Barenboim. 'I'd never heard sounds like it', said Charles. 'I said, "I must try this". So I did. I couldn't keep it up. I remember playing in a performance of Beethoven's *Fifth* one night. It was a wonderful experience, but I couldn't play concentratedly enough to avoid being confused.'

His voice had broken and he sang bass in the chorus. This gave him great pleasure:

> Have you ever sung in a big choir? [he asked Kenneth Harris of *The Observer*]. It's marvellous. I sang in the Bach *B Minor Mass*. There's nothing like it. I don't know whether it's the volume of the voices, or the sense of participation – you're not just listening, you're helping to make the sound – but it's really very exciting. But it's something you can enjoy only if you keep at it. You can't just turn up and say, 'I like singing in choirs. Can I sing in yours tonight, please?'

He sang in Elgar's *Dream of Gerontius* and Benjamin Britten's *Saint Nicholas* of which he says, 'I didn't appreciate it at first. After several rehearsals I began to enjoy it.'
He adds:

> In classical music my taste, such as it is, is conservative. Bach, Mozart and Beethoven. But there are exceptions, such as Berlioz. Once I was listening to Richard Baker's *These You Have Loved* on the BBC. He chose a piece by Berlioz from a choral work I'd never heard of, *L'Enfance du Christ*. I thought I must get it. I play it now often. There's a certain passage in it which is so moving that I'm reduced to tears every time.

Anne was enjoying herself at Benenden. The girls in her circle had responded to the efforts she was now making to be friendly. She soon found that other girls could also be 'a caustic lot', as she says, 'who knew exactly what they thought about other people'. She worked enough at her books to keep out of trouble. But she admits that she never had a favourite subject, except riding. This was a developing, absorbing interest. She rode at school, she rode in the holidays. In the Easter holidays and in the summer before going to Balmoral she competed in Pony Club horse trials, gymkhanas and hunter trials.
At home she kept in touch with her two young brothers and, for a girl who found discipline difficult herself, was surprisingly tough with Andrew when she found him misbehav-

ing. She felt he was getting away with too much, for she remembered discipline being much stricter in her day. But she liked her brothers – 'I am delighted I did not have a sister.'

Prince Andrew was about to start classes under Miss Peebles. A class of about six was arranged, including Lord Linley, Princess Margaret's son. He was also attending gymnastic classes outdoors in Chelsea and learning to ride and swim.

Prince Charles came to London for the state funeral of Sir Winston Churchill in St Paul's Cathedral at the end of January 1965. In June he attended a garden party given by the Queen at Holyroodhouse Palace to meet over five hundred young people, some from the Commonwealth, who were representing universities, sports and youth organizations. Charles made a good impression, being relaxed, friendly and genuinely interested in those he talked with. It surprised his parents, especially his father who thought his son was not good at mixing. The answer was probably that Charles needed a break away from his usual environment so that he could be himself.

Fortunately, that opportunity was soon to come to him. Sir Robert Menzies, for many years the Australian Prime Minister, who had become an elder statesman of the Commonwealth, attended political talks in London that autumn. In conversation with Charles's parents, he helped to promote a plan for Charles to spend six months or so at an Australian school. He would go early the following year, 1966.

His autumn term at Gordonstoun before this break was enlivened by a production of Shakespeare's *Macbeth*. Gordonstoun was not strong on dramatics in his time, but *Macbeth* was something of a ritual there, partly because a significant part of the action takes place nearby at Glamis Castle, the home of the Queen Mother.

Prince Philip in his time had been given only a minor role in the play; but Charles had shown sufficient interest in acting to take on the lead role, that of Macbeth himself. 'It's great fun', he says of acting, 'I love doing it. It gives me great pleasure and having an interest like that keeps one sane I think.'

Rehearsals were spread over six weeks. The Queen and Prince Philip came up from London for the performance on

27 November. There was an audience of over two hundred in the school hall. Even allowing a measure of flattery, Charles, by all accounts, acquitted himself extremely well. For Charles himself, who had not shone at his books or his games, his success meant a great deal. It was a personal triumph – especially in front of his parents.

Before Charles left for the Christmas holidays he was given the silver medal of the Duke of Edinburgh's Award Scheme. There are four qualifications – social service, endurance, craftsmanship, physical fitness. Charles had passed the test in first aid, mountaineering, pottery and running.

After Christmas Prince Philip took Charles and Anne again to Liechtenstein for a ski-ing holiday. Anne also went off for a few days to join some schoolfriends who were ski-ing at Davos in Switzerland and then rejoined her father and brother.

Charles's six months in Australia – he flew there at the end of January 1966 and came back in July – were, by his own emphatic admission, the best thing that had happened in his life. In his radio interview with Jack de Manio on St David's Day, 1969, he said of Timbertop: 'I absolutely adored it. I couldn't have enjoyed it more. The most wonderful experience I've ever had I think. In Australia there is no such thing as aristocracy or anything like that.' Yet he considered Timbertop 'more rigorous and tougher than Gordonstoun'. Of the other boys he said: 'They were very, very good and marvellous people, very genuine. They said exactly what they thought. The only person who took the mickey out of me at all, or, at any rate, made me feel unhappy, I think was an Englishman.' Five years later, in June 1974, in the interviews with Kenneth Harris who asked him what mixing had mattered to him most, Charles replied: 'The time in Australia. More than any other experience, those months opened my eyes. You are judged there on how people see you, and feel about you. There are no assumptions there.'

Initially, the plan was for Charles to spend a term at a school camp on the slopes of Mount Timbertop, in the wilds of the gum tree forests about two hundred miles north of Melbourne. It is used by boys between fourteen and fifteen from the Geelong Church of England Grammar School at Melbourne. Geelong, founded in 1857 when the new country was acquiring wealth and stability, has achieved pre-eminence as *the* school for the sons of wealthy Australians.

It tries hard to re-create the image of an English public school in Australia – too hard, Prince Charles thought. The headmaster when Charles arrived was Mr Thomas Garnett who had been educated at Charterhouse and Cambridge. His predecessor had been Dr Darling, who had taught at Charterhouse.

Dr Darling had been influenced by Kurt Hahn. At Geelong he was responsible for the sons of the rich who would later be exposed to the temptations of self-indulgence. He decided that the best way of dealing with this problem was to set up a tough camp – almost a pioneer camp – well away from the city where boys between the age of fourteen and fifteen would learn to fend for themselves in surroundings not very different from those in which their quite recent forbears had wrested a living.

It is for the political philosophers to ponder on the fact that it has seemed essential in many countries where there is inherited wealth for the privileged sons to be sent on arduous courses that re-create the harsh circumstances of life that are inescapable for those who will inherit little or nothing.

It was in these simulated conditions of reality that Charles was to spend some time. The routine is hard and leaves a lot to the boys. There are about a hundred living in huts which take about fourteen each. Classes are informal and the boys are expected to learn to work on their own. They do all the chores, except the cooking. Wood-chopping is a part of life, to keep the kitchens and winter heating going. 'The first week I was here,' wrote Charles, 'I was made to go out and chop up logs on a hillside in boiling hot weather, I could hardly see my hands for blisters after that!' There was a cross-country run for half an hour twice a week through forest tracks. At the weekends there were arduous expeditions.

All the mountains in the area [reported Charles back to the Gordonstoun *Record*] are very thickly wooded, with equally thick undergrowth down below. When you are walking through the bush you can't see anything except gum tree after gum tree, which tends to become rather monotonous after a time. When choosing a camp-site you have to be very careful where you put your tent as a certain kind of gum sheds its branches without warning. Apart from that you virtually have to inspect every inch of ground you hope to put your tent on in case there are any ants or other ghastly creatures. There is one species of ant called bull ants which are three-quarters of an inch long or more and they bite like mad!

These week-end expeditions were extended as the boys became more experienced. 'The furthest I've been,' said Charles, 'is sixty to seventy miles in three days, climbing about five peaks on the way.'

Sports were equally tough. Apart from swimming, there were tug-o'-war competitions which developed into general scrimmages or races carrying heavy logs. It was not so much organized sports as rough physical competitiveness.

Charles at seventeen was two years older than most of the boys – a very considerable age difference in youth. It gave him a certain sense of seniority. He did not sleep in one of the communal huts, but shared a room in the masters' quarters with an Australian who had been head boy at Geelong and was studying for his university entrance. Charles had decided to take A-levels in French and History the following year and had all the books he wanted with him.

This was the simple pattern of his life. He was away from it all, although inevitably there had to be a detective at Timbertop. He was an Australian detective inspector who had been trained in the Metropolitan Police. Over one hundred miles away there was Squadron Leader David Checketts, one of the Duke of Edinburgh's equerries, who had come out with Charles and had leased a farm where he lived with his wife and three young children. His job was to be there in case of trouble and keep in touch with Buckingham Palace and the Governments in Canberra and London. It turned out to be an easy tour of duty for him.

The press had been catered for with understanding and efficiency. An open day had been arranged for the photographers at Timbertop when Charles arrived with an understanding that then he was to be left alone. It worked.

Charles had looked forward to the experiment, but had had misgivings as to how it would turn out. When the plane carrying him and Checketts had touched down at New York on 28 January, there had been photographers waiting with cries of 'Hiya, prince, wave this way.' Then it was on to San Francisco and the long haul over the Pacific, stopping to refuel at Honolulu. At Sydney he had been met by the Governor-General, Lord Casey, and the then Prime Minister, Mr Holt. He went on to Canberra, the Federal capital, had two quiet days sightseeing and then arrived at Timbertop on 3 February.

Gradually he found that he was happy and contented as he had never been before in his life. The country was wild and daunting; the physical side of life exhausting; problems with his studies he had to work out for himself; home, which had always meant so much to him, was the other side of the world. But he was happy.

When he came to talk later about his months at Timbertop, some of his remarks are quite extraordinary. Here is the Prince of Wales, heir to the throne, bearer of another half dozen grand titles, at the summit of an aristocracy that still has powers, saying with pleasure, 'In Australia there is no such thing as aristocracy or anything like that ... As a matter of fact, having a title, and being a member of the upper classes, can be a hindrance.'

It is as if he had seen through – and disliked – all the deference that is given in Britain, and in the other countries of Europe to a lesser extent, to the bearers of hereditary titles. 'You are judged there on how people see you.' He had passed much of his life among bearers of hereditary titles – at Athens he had been exposed to the full weight of his royal, princely and ducal relatives in Europe – and now in the wilds of Australia he had begun to realize that the titles were meaningless, unless they represented the worth of a man or woman, unless the titles were backed by service. This was an immense step forward in his thinking, and it lends a deep meaning to his remark about Timbertop, 'The most wonderful experience I've ever had, I think.'

It has been said of Australians and New Zealanders that they are the British working-class transported to a new environment which they have had to conquer and adapt to their own desires. There are rich and poor and a majority who lead a good middle sort of life. But they are largely free from the handicap that still hampers Britain and part of Europe – a consciousness of class that, in the case of England, has survived nine hundred years since the alien Normans stamped their rule on a subject people.

Charles's parents considered they had done their best to equip their son for the world by sending him to Cheam and Gordonstoun. But the boys of those two schools had known he was someone apart, and treated him accordingly. Perhaps, it might have been better if, as some had suggested, Charles had been sent to state schools in England instead of expensive private establishments. Perhaps the boys in the state schools would have treated him as the boys did at Timbertop. But it is unlikely. The problems would have been different, but would still have been there.

So it was that Charles had to go to the other side of the world to find himself. As he said, it opened his eyes and 'Australia got me over my shyness.'

At the end of March Charles had a visitor from home – his grandmother, the Queen Mother. She was making an official tour of Australia and Charles was given a long weekend off to meet her at Canberra and spend a couple of days with her in the Snowy Mountains. Charles had a lot to tell her, including the fact that he would like to stay a second term at Timbertop. The option had been left open to him.

Before the end of the first term Charles went with a group of thirty boys and the headmaster to visit the Anglican missionary centres in Papua, New Guinea. The trip had become part of the Geelong tradition. The party flew by way of Brisbane to Port Moresby and then went by launch to the village of Wedau, near Dogura Cathedral. There was a great welcome on the beach by the feather-adorned warriors and their women wearing grass skirts. Charles stayed there for four days, seeing all aspects of the missionary and welfare work, taking communion with over one thousand others in the Cathedral, joining in native feasts and dancing. Charles wrote an essay after the visit and ended:

Lastly I would like to mention how fresh and sincere I found the Church at Dogura. Everyone was so eager to take part in the services, and the singing was almost deafening. One felt that it might almost be the original Church. Where Christianity is new, it must be much easier to enter into the whole spirit of it wholeheartedly, and it is rather wonderful that you can still go somewhere where this strikes you.

In the holiday between terms Charles saw more of Australia. With Squadron Leader Checketts he visited a cattle ranch in Queensland, saw Sydney and went to the Outward Bound School on the Hawkesbury River. He stayed with families and everyone enjoyed having him around.

The second term at Timbertop was in June and July, the Australian winter months, and there was enough snow for Charles to go ski-ing and to give a few hints to the beginners. There was even more wood-chopping, but Charles found time to go for long walks on his own, fished a little and worked at his books. They were good days.

But the end of term came and the end of Charles's first Australian experience. Royal messages tend to be filtered and edited, but Charles's farewell to the country had a ring of sincerity: 'It would be difficult to leave without saying how much I have enjoyed and appreciated my stay in Australia ... I am sad to be leaving; and yet I shall now be able to visualize Australia in the most vivid terms, after such a marvellous visit.'

Charles had a good journey back with David Checketts. They stopped off at Auckland to have a brief look at New

Zealand, touched down at Tahiti, and then flew on to Mexico City for a few days. The British Ambassador, with whom they stayed, had laid on a useful programme. By now some of Charles's interests were becoming known and he was given an informed tour of some of the great monuments of the Aztec civilization. There were lunches, a dance and a few small receptions.

Charles then flew on to Jamaica and met his father and sister. They all attended the Commonwealth Games which were taking place there, and Anne celebrated her sixteenth birthday. It was a time for agreeable relaxation in the sunshine of the Caribbean.

Anne took her O-levels this year and did quite well. She passed in English Language, English Literature (with an A mark), French, History, Geography and Biology. She failed in Latin. In mathematics it was thought best to enter her for the fairly easy Royal Society of Arts test in Arithmetic, which she passed.

5
A Double Launching

By the time Charles came back with his father and sister, there was only a shortened holiday with the Queen, Prince Andrew and Prince Edward at Balmoral. There were visits from German relatives, now an established custom during the summer. It was noticed that Prince Charles had changed in the seven months he had been away. He knew his own mind more. He talked freely about his experiences to the family and friends, even if he kept some of his thoughts to himself. Anne, too, at sixteen, was changing. Riding was still the great passion, but she was beginning to take some interest in clothes and make-up, and was something of a flirt.

Charles was to spend another year at Gordonstoun and take his two A-levels. Anne had another two years to go at Benenden and would probably also take A-levels.

Charles also knew by now that he had won an important point and would be going to university before he spent some years with the services. He had made it quite clear in the months before he went to Australia that this was what he wanted to do.

As a result of his views, the Queen and Prince Philip had organized a dinner at Buckingham Palace where the opinions of some important men could be heard. The guests were Mr (later Sir) Harold Wilson, the Prime Minister, Dr Ramsey, Archbishop of Canterbury, Lord Mountbatten, almost inevitably, Sir Charles Wilson, Principal of Glasgow University and at the time Chairman of the Committee of University Vice-Chancellors, and Dr Woods, Dean of Windsor, and as such close to the Queen as her domestic chaplain. Sir Michael (later

Lord) Adeane, the Queen's Principal Private Secretary, was at the dinner to take notes. The five guests mulled over the future of Charles until very late in the evening. It was later called 'the sounding of five wise men', though some outside the deliberations might have questioned the adjective. Prince Charles was not present.

According to Prince Philip, who later gave a full account of the proceedings, advice was asked of the guests if they thought it was good for Charles to go to a university, and if they did which university and what subjects he should study. In retrospect, it all seems rather superfluous though, no doubt, the guests enjoyed the dinner, the wines, and the opportunity to give their views.

It was solemnly decided that it would be an advantage for Charles to go to a university. As for the choice between universities, the 'red-brick' and post-war universities were soon ruled out. As between Oxford and Cambridge, the latter was the favourite.

In fact, that is where Charles wanted to go. His cousins Prince William and Prince Richard of Gloucester had been there and Charles had visited them and liked what he saw. Sandringham is not far from Cambridge and Charles felt at home in that countryside. Also, in his visits to Cambridge Charles had been impressed by the beauty of the colleges and their surroundings.

When Charles went back to Gordonstoun in the autumn of 1966, he knew he would be going to Cambridge. Which college he would enter and what he would study had not yet been decided.

Back at Gordonstoun Charles was head of his house, Windmill Lodge, and found that after Australia many matters which had loomed large in the past now seemed rather trivial. In a way he had outgrown Gordonstoun. He put up with it because he knew it was his last year. He liked some of the masters and boys. He wanted to get his two A-levels so that no one could say he was going to Cambridge without the qualifications asked of others.

He broke his nose playing rugby, and an injury or two at rugger never does any schoolboy's prestige any harm.

He was eighteen on 14 November, and although he spent the day at school and had no more than an evening coffee and cake party with his friends, the event did have a certain significance in his life.

Under the Regency Act passed in 1953 he was now entitled to reign as king without a regency should his mother abdicate or die. Under the 1953 Act Prince Philip would have acted as regent until Charles was eighteen if his wife had abdicated, died or been unable to carry out her duties. From now on, if his mother was unable to reign, Charles would be regent. In broad terms, the regent has the same powers as the monarch.

On his eighteenth birthday Charles also became the senior of the four adult members of the royal family who act as counsellors of state in the absence of the Queen abroad, or if she is sick. They can perform certain duties including signing papers and holding privy council meetings.

Charles's financial position also improved. When he became Duke of Cornwall on his mother's accession to the throne in 1952, he was given £10,000 a year out of the revenues until he was eighteen. Now it was increased to £30,000 a year, although the money would still be administered by the Queen.

While Charles was at school this term his mother asked Dr Woods, the Dean of Windsor, to visit Cambridge and advise which college would be most suitable for Charles. He came back with a short-list of five, but recommended Trinity. It is one of the great Cambridge colleges, with a high reputation for learning and drawing nearly three-quarters of its undergraduates from grammar, rather than public schools. The new Master was none other than 'Rab', now Lord Butler, who had held most of the great offices of state in Conservative adminstrations, but had been deprived of the prime ministership on two occasions by a cabal of the Tory hierarchy, 'the magic circle'. He came of a long line of famous Cambridge scholars and had gone to Trinity where he might ponder on the follies of Westminster, administer a great royal foundation and, as it now turned out, help to guide the education of the heir to the throne. As a senior minister he was well-known to the Queen and Prince Philip.

Charles's grandfather, King George VI, had been a Trinity man, though he had not been allowed to enjoy a full university life. So was the Dean of Windsor, who had been sent to spy out the land. His son, Edward, was also at Trinity.

As the Queen and Prince Philip decided that to Trinity Charles should go an announcement to that effect was made to the press on 4 December. He was to enter Cambridge in October 1967, the next year.

It was a quiet Christmas for the royal family at the end of 1966 and there were no ski-ing holidays in Europe for Charles and Anne. Charles had now only two terms more at Gordonstoun. He was made head boy as his father had been before him. At Gordonstoun the title was 'Guardian', just as the head of a house was called a 'Helper'. The ranks, or distinctions, are taken from Plato's *Republic*. In that ideal state the 'Guardians' form the ruling class and are assisted by the 'Helpers' or 'Auxiliaries'. In calling it an 'ideal state', it is not necessary to approve of it. To many Plato's *Republic* is a nauseating fascist organization. However, at Gordonstoun, the titles were retained as a compliment to the founder, Kurt Hahn. In effect, 'Guardian' and 'Helpers' carried out much the same tasks as head boy and prefects in the traditional English school. Perhaps the 'Guardian' at Gordonstoun was expected to show more understanding of the boys' problems than a head boy. He also had no punitive powers, such as beating. Charles, being a humane young man, made the job more that of a spokesman of the boys to the authorities.

In April Anne had a pleasant break. She joined a party at Nice to see the International Horse Show. She was now a sufficiently experienced horsewoman to take pleasure in the finer points of the contest. It made her all the more determined to reach the same standards.

On 1 May an announcement was made about the studies Charles would pursue at Cambridge. They were his decision.

He would read for an arts degree in archaeology and physical and social anthropology.

When the time came for me to go to Cambridge [Charles explained later] and choose my subjects, I thought: 'now here's a chance I'll never have again – to do some pre-history, get to know about the earlier societies, and the most primitive kinds of men'. When you meet as many people as I do, from different countries, different colours, different stages of social development, with different drives, you become curious about what makes men tick differently. You wonder about the fundamental tension in a man, in mankind, between body and soul. I got on to this at Gordonstoun and I grabbed the chance to follow it up at Cambridge.

Before Charles left Gordonstoun in the summer, he had a chance to play a comic role on the stage. The Queen has a highly developed sense of humour – a satirical humour expressed in pointed mimicry. It is probably a safety-valve, releasing emotions pent-up in her immaculate public appearances. Charles has inherited it. His humour developed out of the Crazy Gang into the Goons and the Monty Python worlds. A mad, surrealist universe, tough, barbed and, as they say, zany. If it lacks the subtlety of *Alice in Wonderland* – well, subtlety is not for today.

Gordonstoun was putting on Gilbert and Sullivan's *The Pirates of Penzance*, a satire on three Victorian institutions – the army, the police and the Englishman's sense of duty.

Charles was to sing the role of the Pirate King.

It was a very jolly performance with much applause from the audience, which included the Queen and Prince Philip. Charles looked appropriately fierce and piratical and sang with feeling such lines as:

> Oh, better far to live and die
> Under the brave black flag I fly,
> Than play a sanctimonious part,

> With a pirate head and a pirate heart.
> Away to the cheating world you go
> Where pirates are well-to-do;
> But I'll be true to the song I sing.
> For I am a pirate king.

In July Charles sat for his A-levels in French and History. He passed and did particularly well in History. An official said later that he had shone in his optional history paper. He got a distinction, a standard reached by only six per cent of the four thousand candidates.

It was the end of Charles's school-days – the end of the trail that had led from Hill House in Knightsbridge, Cheam in Berkshire, Gordonstoun in Morayshire, and Timbertop in New South Wales.

'I didn't enjoy school as much as I might have', Charles has said, 'but that was only because I'm happier at home than anywhere else.' Nevertheless, he looks back with nostalgia to the months at Timbertop, thousands of miles from home. But then Timbertop was to Charles not so much a school as a liberating experience.

In August Charles and Anne joined their father at Cowes for the yachting. Sea-sickness detracted a lot of the enjoyment of sailing from both Charles and Anne. But they did their duty and the social life, afloat and ashore, at Cowes is exhilarating. Then it was on to Balmoral for the holidays.

For Charles, the next stage was Cambridge. It is a privilege for any young man or woman to attend university. It is an even greater privilege to be chosen for Oxford or Cambridge. Most who have read for a degree there look back all their life on those years as containing something special in quality. Since the war the two universities have maintained their standards. Only the brightest young men and women are chosen and money and social position as qualifications have become less influential. Traditions are upheld and the undergraduates spend their three years or more in an atmosphere of cultured ease attached to colleges that are in many cases a heritage of architectural beauty. Charles's A-levels were not outstanding and there was some grumbling that if it were not for his position they would not have earned him a place at Cambridge. This was to misjudge the situation. Charles's position was so special that not to have given him the opportunity of going to Cambridge, when he wanted to, would have been churlish and stupid. He needed the best in education for the job he had been born to.

Lord Butler had a meeting with the British and international press before Charles took up residence in October. He was to live in college with the other undergraduates. Lord Butler considered it essential that he made friends and went out for a drink with them rather than sit alone in his rooms.

Charles was given rooms first on the second-floor of New Court and then later in Great Court. Undergraduate rooms consist of a small bedroom, a study and a small cubby, generally fitted with not much more than a gas-ring, though Charles later had some more extensive kitchen equipment installed. Like other undergraduates who could afford it, Charles had some of his own furniture brought in – not a lot, and not lavish, but enough to give the rooms a personal style. Bathrooms are rare in the older colleges, but Charles was somewhat privileged; there was a bathroom on his staircase, shared by about half a dozen.

The three terms of the year are short, about eight weeks each, leaving a very long summer vacation. It is tempting, but unwise, to abandon studies during that period. It gives an opportunity to read the books that it is so easy to neglect during the terms, full as they are of opportunities for sport and mixing in the innumerable societies and clubs.

Undergraduate dress was becoming increasingly casual, if not eccentric during his years, but he stuck to the traditional post-war pattern of corduroy trousers and sports jacket. He wore, as is the rule, the short gown of the undergraduate and, like most, used a bicycle to get around.

He had passed his driving test and bought his first car, an MG, at the end of the year. The rule was that no one under twenty-two should keep a car in the university, so Charles kept his on the outskirts of the city.

The routine of Charles's day was soon established. He made himself coffee or tea and had a light breakfast in his rooms; attended lectures, given in various college halls, in the mornings; as often as not had lunch in hall; in the afternoons there was either sport or reading in a library; dinner in hall was obligatory on most evenings; there were essays to prepare which had to be read to tutors who would then discuss them, an experience which can be daunting even to the brightest. Apart from all this there was the mixing that is essential if the best is to be derived from the years at university. The pattern is exciting, exhilarating, and can be exhausting.

His tutor at Trinity, whose task was to have an overall guidance of Charles, was Mr Denis Marrian, an organic chemist, and there was soon an easy, warm relationship between them. Undergraduate friends were easy to find. At Trinity there was Edward Woods, son of the Dean of Windsor; there was James Buxton who was related to Aubrey Buxton, naturalist, TV producer and friend of Prince Philip, who appointed him an extra equerry. The friendship with James Buxton became close and they were members of the same dining club which from time to time would put on dinner jackets and eat, drink and be merry. Aubrey Buxton's daughter, Cindy, was also at Cambridge doing a secretarial course. Charles struck up a friendship with her and took her out occasionally.

Trinity, indeed the Master, Lord Butler, gave Charles the opportunity of meeting a girl who was to play a considerable part in his life for some time. She was Lucia Santa Cruz, daughter of a former Chilean ambassador to London. She was beautiful and clever with a degree from London University, a Ph.D from Oxford and was at Cambridge doing research for Lord Butler on his memoirs. She was four years older than Charles, dressed well and was extremely attractive. Charles continued to see her and take her out years after he left Cambridge. In 1975 she got married.

Charles made friends with two undergraduates on the same staircase in New Court. On the same floor was 'Nick' Jenkins, who was a subaltern in the Greenjackets and was reading classics under the army university scholarship scheme. Under

Charles lived Hywel Jones, who came from a working-class family in Cardiff and was reading economics. 'It was difficult at first', said Jones, 'because I didn't want him to think I was talking to him just because he was Prince of Wales. I think it was more a barrier on my side than his.' The barrier was more or less overcome, however, and they had many discussions, especially on Wales. These were a help to Charles for he knew he would soon be spending some time in the principality before his investiture as Prince of Wales when he was twenty-one in 1969, now only two years away.

A link between Charles, 'Nick' Jenkins and Hywel Jones was that all three were members of the Trinity amateur acting group, the Dryden Society.

Charles had his luxuries. A farmhouse had been refurbished for him on the nearby royal estate at Sandringham and at week-ends if he felt like it he could go over and relax with a friend. In the shooting season he would come back with some game he had shot and offer a brace here and there, with the least ostentatiousness possible.

He could not be entirely free from the Palace and his royal responsibilities, although David Cheketts had now been appointed to look after all the Prince's routine matters and tried to leave him free to live his Cambridge life.

There was, however, one important early interruption. The Queen thought it was time that both Prince Charles and Princess Anne attended the state opening of parliament on 31 October. This is the most significant constitutional act in the monarch's year. Though the speech from the throne is composed by the Government, the reality of the British political way of life is enshrined in the ceremony when the sovereign appears, surrounded by all the panoply of state, before the Lords and Commons and announces another session of Parliament. For Charles and Anne it was a ceremonial initiation into the workings of the British constitution and the part the royal family plays in it. For the Lords and Commons, and the nation at large, the presence of the Prince and Princess, now approaching adulthood, was a visible sign of the emergence of a new generation, which would in turn take on its responsibilities.

In the new year, 1968, Charles was asked to write an article for *Varsity*, the undergraduate magazine, giving his reactions to life at Cambridge. He responded with a graceful and amusing piece of which all that seemed to strike the imagination of Fleet Street was that he complained at being woken up early by the dustman making a clatter under his windows.

Anne was looking forward to leaving Benenden in July. Not because she had been unhappy at school, but she would be eighteen in August and it was time for her to spread her wings. She was going to take A-levels in History and Geography, but was not working particularly hard for them. She had no intention of going to university, 'I think it's a very much over-rated pastime', she said in her blunt way.

She was pinning her hopes on becoming a first-class horsewoman. In the spring Mrs Hatton-Hall, her instructor, thought that it was time for Anne to have more specialized training. So Mrs Alison Oliver, wife of a very well-known show jumper, was brought in. Alison Oliver was one of the best instructors in the country and her services much-prized. Her stables were at Brookfield Farm, near Warfield Park, conveniently close to Windsor, and it was there that Anne was going to spend much of her spare time in future.

Faithful and much-loved High Jinks was put out to grass. It was time to move from a pony to a horse. The Crown Equerry suggested to Alison Oliver that Purple Star, an offspring of his ex-Olympic mare, Stella, might fit the bill. He did. He was a 15.3-hand bay gelding, who had done a little hunting, but was otherwise untried. He was not, perhaps, big enough for someone as tall as Anne, but he had a lot of personality and promised well. He proved a challenge to Anne, and she enjoyed it. He was mettlesome, had moods and took a lot of riding. But he was highly intelligent and quick. He opened up another chapter in Anne's life.

In April she passed her driving test without difficulty. Like Charles she was helped by the fact that for years she had been learning to drive on the private roads of the family estates. She had to wait, however, until October for her first car, a blue Rover 2000, a belated eighteenth birthday present, and then begin her career as a driver – which was not to be without its problems.

In the summer Anne took her A-levels. She passed, but not well, with a Grade D in History and a Grade E in Geography. Charles also had exams at the end of his first Cambridge year and did well – much, they say, to the relief of his tutors. He obtained an upper second class in the first part of his tripos, archaeology and anthropology, which was a sixty-six per cent pass.

One of the more stimulating aspects of his studies had been a short period of practical archaeological work earlier in the year. He joined a small party of other Oxbridge students in France and the Channel Islands. His father flew him out to Bordeaux at the end of March and he had a few days in the Dordogne studying the famous Lascaux cave wall-paintings, now closed to most visitors because of deterioration, and then went on to Brittany to see Celtic remains. In Jersey he joined in a dig in the La Cotte cave.

Charles had reason to be pleased with his first year's results. The word began to be passed around Cambridge that he was an able and assiduous worker. 'A boy who worked so hard could not have failed.'

He went to the Trinity May Ball on 10 June and the following week made his first official appearance at Royal Ascot, riding in the first carriage with the Queen and Prince Philip. In July both Charles and Anne attended one of the Garden Parties at Buckingham Palace.

Charles was now given what he had long wanted – the chance to learn to fly. A first-class instructor, Squadron Leader Philip Pinney, a New Zealander, who was at the Central Flying School at Little Rissington in Somerset, was transferred to the Queen's Flight at RAF Benson in Oxfordshire. He was given the task of teaching Charles, and on 30 July they went up for thirty minutes in a Chipmunk trainer. The plan was for Charles to put in as much time as he could without interfering with his studies.

During his first long vacation his father had organized a strenuous programme for him in August to widen his experience of life. He visited seven government departments and made twenty-five brief visits to see men at work. In South Wales he was shown how safety at work was studied and developed. In London he went underground to see the tunnel being bored for the new Victoria Line by a specialized team of workers, mainly Irish. He visited the police. In Edinburgh he was shown how a newspaper is produced by the editor of the Edinburgh *Evening News*. He visited Welbeck Colliery in Nottinghamshire and afterwards the general manager, Mr Wilf Barrett, said, 'He's a bloody grand lad with a hell of a sense of humour.'

As if this was not enough Charles was studying Welsh affairs and had bought a Welsh language course on records. He was doing some ground work before spending a term at the University of Wales at Aberystwyth the following year.

For Anne, little did she know it, this was a year of destiny. She met her future husband, Mark Phillips, for the first time. It was in the Whitbread wine-cellar in the City where a reception was being given in honour of those who had taken part in the Mexico Olympic Games. Anne's grandmother, the Queen Mother, took her along. It was not a case of love at first sight, but horses provided a common interest.

In September Anne, tired of being told of her inadequate French by her family, enrolled for a six-week intensive course at the Berlitz School of Languages in London. Berlitz do not believe in wasting their time or your money. It was five days a week from 9 am to 6.45 pm. As is usual with her when she has made up her mind, she saw it through.

Anne's main task this autumn was to get herself ready to be launched on the world in 1969. School-days were over, official duties loomed ahead. She had to start worrying about clothes. She had to slim down. She had to get used to having a lady-in-waiting and an office at Buckingham Palace where her life was organized. As her parents pointed out, she now had a job to do.

Anne did slim successfully – mainly, she says, by eating less.

She emerged with a presentable, trim figure and well-shaped legs. This last quality was of immense importance for a young woman at the time. For this was the age of the mini-skirt. It could be said that this fashion, started in England, was one of the most significant trends in women's clothes ever developed. It swept the world. The French, for so long the undisputed leaders in feminine fashion, could not conceal their anger, at first criticized it as stupid and vulgar, and ended up by having to copy it. It had something to do with the increased freedom of women; it had something to do with the changes in sexual behaviour; it had something to do with the revolt of young girls against their mothers for it was a fashion that best suited the young, it also suited English girls because they tend to be slim and have well-shaped legs. It must be said that the fashion livened up the scene and was provocative to men. At the height of the fashion, with the skirt becoming higher and higher, dresses became little more than tunics.

As a relief from the mini-skirt, trousers began to be worn by women. Instead of showing a lot of leg, they showed no leg at all and the sexual provocativeness was limited to the shaping of the rear. It became fashionable to wear trouser suits for evening wear. Later trousers, led by jeans, became almost a uniform for many girls during the day.

These were the fashions prevalent when Anne found herself about to be launched on the world. But there were other changes than style. Until Anne's generation, the young girls whose parents were rich would have gone to a very fashionable dressmaker or couturier. The habit was dying out. Partly because taxation was reducing the money available except among the very rich; partly because there was an almost instinctive trend to a more democratic appearance. The age of ostentation had passed. Anne was conscious of all this. In many ways it suited her personality. A girl who was happiest in a jumper and jodhpurs, who rejected overt femininity, was not likely to worry too much about clothes. 'People say one's a bit square', she remarked, 'well, fine ... I've never pretended to be anything else.'

However, she was Princess Anne, would be taking her part

in innumerable public events, and had to be a credit to her family and to the country. Pictures of her would be studied, not only here, but throughout the world and, in the modern climate of opinion, views about her appearance would be freely published. To a certain extent, a princess was expected to be a leader of fashion. Anne was not unmindful of clothes. She like to look presentable. But they did not, never could, play a big part in her life. She is just not that sort of woman.

However, she started going on shopping expeditions. She bought off-the-peg clothes in the big stores and boutiques in Bond Street, Knightsbridge and the King's Road. Some were disastrous; some a success. Her mother gave her opinion when asked – sometimes when not asked. Anne is nobody's fool. She knew within what limits she could choose clothes for official engagements.

Like most of her generation she detested hats. But hats would have to be worn. As it happened, the hated hats turned out to be one of the most successful and original aspects of her appearance. The favourable comments encouraged her and, in time, she found herself almost interested in choosing a design that would set tongues wagging. There was a great variety, but perhaps the must successful in her early years was a sombrero worn at a rakish angle. Within days the shops were full of them. At last, Anne was giving them a lead.

Anne has good features, fine eyes, a well-shaped strong nose. Her mouth is full and generous, but the lower lip is prominent and tends to give a heaviness to her chin. Unfortunately, she tends to frown naturally and this comes out in her photographs – even when she is not annoyed with the photographers. At this time of her life, however, she had the freshness of youth, which has its own magic, and she seemed determined to do her best in the world of official engagements that awaited her.

As 1969 approached, the year that was to see a wider life for Anne and the investiture of Charles at Caernarvon, both were lucky in many ways. Their parents were loving and there to help; outside the family the people of Great Britain and many other countries associated in the Commonwealth were waiting to give them a cheer on their way.

6
Prince of Wales

In January 1969, Charles made his first solo flight. Squadron Leader Pinney had found him an enthusiastic pupil in the Chipmunk trainer. As Charles remarked later:

> I always thought I was going to be terrified. I was dreading the moment when I was going to have to go up [alone]. But the day I went on my solo the instructor taxied to the end of the runway, having landed, and suddenly climbed out and said, 'You're on your own, mate!' And I only had time to have a few butterflies in my tummy and then I taxied off, wondering if I could do it ... and the moment I was in the air it was marvellous.

His studies were going well. His tutor, Dr Denis Marrian, said 'Quite frankly it is a delight to talk about the Prince because I do not have to flannel at all. He really is doing well here.' Dr Robert Robson, who supervised the studies in political and economic history with which Charles was completing his degree, commented: 'A really striking aspect about the Prince is the speed at which he works. He has always been thorough, but he now has the ability to organize his work, assimilating facts for his essays and assembling them quickly and clearly. This is a sign of true intelligence.'

It was not all work. On 7 February, he helped to judge the Cambridge Rag Queen. She was Susan Francis, twenty, an undergraduate at Girton, and Charles crowned her. He was also rehearsing hard for the Trinity Review, *Revulution*, which was to have half a dozen performances at the end of February. Charles was appearing in sixteen of the forty sketches.

'The Prince has good timing', said the undergraduate producer, John Parry, 'and he ad-libs well when fellow-actors dry
up on stage and he doesn't giggle at his own jokes on stage like
a lot of student actors.'

'Most of the jokes,' said Charles talking of the forthcoming
show, 'are the most awful sort of groan jokes, you know.' They
were. He walked off stage with a pretty girl saying, 'I like to
give myself airs.' He came on and said defiantly, 'I wreak
vengeance', and another actor passed in front of him holding
his nose saying, 'So that's what it is!' But the sketch that
attracted the world press was Charles sitting in a dustbin and
being interviewed about an undergraduate called 'Reg Sprott'
– a more or less amusing comment on his article in *Varsity*
complaining about the noise the dustman made in the early
morning.

Charles enjoyed it all enormously. He says, 'I'd probably
have been committed to an institution long ago were it not for
the ability to see the funny side of life.'

Saturday 1 March was St David's Day. The national day
of Wales turned out important both for Anne and Charles.
Prince Philip, as Colonel-in-Chief of the Welsh Guards, would
normally have presented the traditional leeks to the regiment
on that day. As he was unable to attend, Princess Anne was
given the job and went down to Pirbright to carry out her first
public engagement.

Charles's first radio interview was broadcast on the same
day by the BBC. The interviewer was Jack de Manio, an experienced broadcaster who has the gift of drawing people out
by sympathy rather than by bullying. When the question of an
interview was discussed Charles suggested de Manio, but it
was not entirely coincidental that de Manio, like David Checketts, was a director of the public relations firm, Neilson
McCarthy, who certainly deserve the royal warrant and coat-
of-arms awarded to the providers of goods and services to the
royal family.

The interview was a great success. Charles talked about his
education with frankness and charm. He said that at Cambridge he at first played a lot of music, but had then spent

more time acting. 'Regrettably I've had to neglect my cello, which is very bad I must say, because I do enjoy it enormously.'

These were the years of the great student demos not only here, but world-wide, especially in the United States and France. Charles showed that he had spent some time thinking about this development.

'I can't help feeling that because students and many people feel so helpless and anonymous in life and society that demonstrating is one useful way of making known your own particular opinions about world affairs, and domestic affairs and things like that.'

On his forthcoming term at Aberystwyth and his investiture he commented:

It would be unnatural if one didn't feel any apprehension about it. But I think if one takes it as it comes it'll be much easier. I expect at Aberystwyth there may be one or two demonstrations and as long as I don't get covered too much in egg and tomato I'll be all right. I've hardly been to Wales, and you can't expect people to be overzealous about the fact of having a so-called English Prince to come amongst them and be frightfully excited.

The Guardian, no slavish adulator of the monarchy, commented on the interview:

A young man who can talk to the British public in its present iconoclastic mood without being either pompous at one extreme or undignified at the other has qualities to be admired. He will need them this year as he appears to be well aware. His investiture as Prince of Wales will be ritualistic in an age which dislikes ceremony, traditional at a time when people want something new, authoritarian when respect for authority is crumbling and English in character before people who are feeling very Welsh. By accepting that there will be demonstrations, and trying to understand why, Prince Charles has already done something to disarm them. What will the demonstrations be about? It so happens that

the investiture comes with the floodtide of Celtic nationalism.

Charles had every reason to feel some apprehension. Welsh
nationalism had indeed grown considerably in the ten years
since the Queen had announced that her eldest son would be
invested as Prince of Wales at Caernarvon.

Plaid Cymru, the nationalist party, had steadily grown in
numbers. Its aims were some measure of independence from
England. There were also groups of extremists, including the
Free Wales Army, who embarked on a series of acts of sabo-
tage and bombings. On 17 November 1967 there was a heavy
explosion causing £30,000 of damage at the Temple of Peace
at Cardiff where four hundred and fifty Welsh representatives
had gathered to discuss the arrangements for the investiture.
There were seven more explosions during 1968. There were
more to come in 1969 before the investiture took place on 1
July. There was certainly enough potential trouble around to
worry the police and the Special Branch.

While Charles was bracing himself for the challenge of
his year, Anne was tackling the series of public engagements
arranged for her and stretching months ahead. Now that she
had her own car she drove down as often as she could to Alison
Oliver's stables – public life was not going to divert her from
her riding. In April she went on a ski-ing holiday to Val
d'Isère, a fashionable resort in the French Alps. She spent ten
days there with a party of around a dozen young people, enjoyed it, and made some progress on her skis.

Charles, at any rate on the surface, was very relaxed. He
played polo for the Cambridge team, though, as he admitted,
there was not much competition for a place as it was a rich
young man's sport. He enjoys polo. 'I love the game. I love the
ponies. I love the exercise. It's also the one team game I can
play.'

Over a period he entertained his family in his rooms. The
Queen and Prince Philip came for lunch, Anne for dinner, the
Queen Mother for tea and Lord Mountbatten for a buffet
when he met some of Charles's friends.

Charles was somewhat surprised one day to see his tutor, Dr Marrian, coming up from a grating in a college court. 'I was just staggering up the steps from this very dirty cellar (a wine cellar)', Marrian later explained. 'Oh!' said Charles, 'I've often wondered where the senior tutor lived.'

Charles arrived for his term at the University of Wales on 20 April. The Chipmunk trainer and his instructor were based nearby at Aberporth RAF station so that he could continue with his flying. Aberystwyth is a pleasant seaside resort which lies on the shores of Cardigan Bay. He was given a normal room in the Pant-y-Celyn hall of residence and settled down to study Welsh history, literature and its difficult language. Charles surprised the Welsh by the knowledge of the language he had already acquired and by his accent, which is no mean feat for anyone who has been brought up with English as the mother tongue. The registrar, Arfon Owen, said, 'No one but a gifted mimic could have learned to pronounce it so well.'

'I worked for eight years on my Welsh', said Charles afterwards, 'and it was damned hard – it's a hard language, very rich and very complex – but I enjoyed it and when I met my Aberystwyth tutor the other day (that was five years later), he was quite pleased with what I remembered and with my accent.'

A few weeks after his arrival he made a five-minute speech in Welsh at the National Eisteddfod of the Urdd in the town. It had a great reception and made him many friends among the Welsh, who, proud as they are, have a great heart.

His assiduousness at his studies and his relaxed manner when he met the other students – and he made sure there were many opportunities – were admirable, taking into account a sinister background which could not be lightly dismissed even if it were caused by only an isolated group of fanatics.

There were threats to assassinate him. There were insults hurled, derogatory songs sung and even a record produced. 'This German oaf' was among the epithets.

The authorities took every precaution. A bomb disposal expert was brought in. The police were strengthened and nearly a hundred Special Branch officers, an élite force, were stationed in the town. The risk of an attack by a fanatic or two is so incalculable, however, that no precautions can be adequate. This was the nightmare of the authorities.

Charles freely admits to 'having butterflies in my tummy' at moments of stress, but he gave no outward sign and, by the qualities of his own personality, won over the students, Aberystwyth and many Welsh beyond. It was a triumph, a personal triumph, for an overt public relations exercise would have been counter-productive among the highly intelligent and wary Welsh sharing his life at the university.

The shy, introverted boy of Cheam and Gordonstoun had come a long way.

Whilst he was in Wales Charles was appointed Colonel-in-Chief of the Regiment of Wales, which had been newly formed under an army amalgamation scheme. He presented the regiment with its new colours and was to wear its uniform at his investiture. Anne was also given an army appointment. She was made Colonel-in-Chief of the 14/20th King's Hussars, a tank regiment. In April President Saragat of Italy paid a state visit and before the official banquet Anne was to attend the Queen gave her the Family Order, a miniature of the Queen surrounded by small diamonds and worn on the left shoulder in evening dress.

In May she was to go with her parents on a state visit to Austria. She went down with influenza a few days before the trip, but made a quick recovery and flew out two days after the Queen and Prince Philip. It was an agreeable tour with visits to Salzburg and Innsbruck, but for Anne the most memorable event was riding one of the Lipizzaner stallions in the Spanish Riding School, a charming baroque building in Vienna. The school's complicated discipline, which takes both horses and riders years to learn, enshrines a highly elaborate form of equestrianism which has been preserved since the Renaissance. Knowing the tastes of the Queen and her daughter the Austrians gave two Haflinger ponies as one of their gifts.

Anne was also kept busy elsewhere, visiting the Rover Company at Solihull, going to Wembley for the FA Cup Final, launching a giant tanker, ss *Esso Northumbria* on Tyneside, opening the Festival of London Stores, and visiting an RSPCC centre in Edinburgh. On 28 June she flew to Paris for a ball given by the British Ambassador, Mr (later Sir) Christopher Soames, and his wife for their two children, Nicholas, twenty-one, and Emma, eighteen. The magnificent British Embassy was a scene of splendour and invitations had been relentlessly pursued by Paris society.

Charles had left Aberystwyth on 22 June, not much more than a week before the ceremony in Caernarvon Castle. He was now the central figure in a meticulously planned programme, worked out over two years, which was to be the greatest public event of the British monarchy since the coronation of the Queen in 1953. Everything was falling into place with unerring precision to show not only Wales and the rest of Britain, but the Commonwealth and the world, that the organization surrounding the monarchy was in a class of its own.

A week before the investiture a film of one hour fifty minutes, *Royal Family*, a joint BBC and ITV venture, was put on the air and seen on its first showing by twenty-three million people. It was repeated a week later and seen by fifteen millions, of whom six millions had already seen the first showing. Shorter versions were sold to many countries overseas. A particularly valuable sale was made to the USA, valuable in terms of money, even more valuable in terms of publicity.

Filming had gone on intermittently from June 1968 to May 1969 in over a hundred and fifty locations. There was a risk in the showing of the film, as the Queen recognized. An element of magic and a certain remoteness are an essential part of the mystique of monarchy. On the other hand, the advantages of communicating to Britain and the world that the Queen and her family were agreeable persons who did a job, but also enjoyed their leisure, were very great indeed in a world where public interest was largely engineered by the media and the advertisers.

The whole family took part. The children were an essential part of the 'happy family' image that bears the stamp of approval of the creators of public opinion. Charles, Anne, Andrew and Edward were seen at work and play. Their natural acting ability was enhanced by brilliant camera work and production. The film was a great success and the sniping was mainly confined to the smart sharpshooters of the intelligentsia.

There was much more than this to the publicity campaign. During the year Charles had had a series of photographic sessions showing him in just about every role. It was an exhausting business for the photographers, however polite, were demanding. Over five hundred pictures were selected and sent to the Palace. Finally, with the Queen taking part in the choice, seventy pictures were approved and released to the world press.

David Frost, who, whether you like him or not, is the most famous interviewer in the world, made with Prince Charles an hour-long film which was released to the cinema circuits on 4 July, just after the investiture, thus leaving the first bite of the cherry to the television programmes covering the event.

On 26 June, Charles appeared in a thirty-minute TV programme, organized jointly by the BBC and ITV, in which he was interviewed by Cliff Michelmore and Brian Connell, two of television's famous names. Among the questions and answers were:

Q. How much influence has your father on you?
   Is he as tough a disciplinarian inside the Palace as he appears to be outside on occasion?
A. Does he appear to be a tough disciplinarian?
Q. Yes, he does. Well, he seems to tell people what they ought to be doing – sit down and shut up. Has he ever said that to you?
A. The whole time, yes. It's very good for me, I think anyway. Yes, I think he has had quite an influence on me – I think particularly in my younger days. Now I'm becoming a bit more independent. I think I may be slightly late in development. I'm not sure.

Q. Charles was asked what the investiture would mean to him.

A. I think it will probably mean quite a lot. I think on the whole I will be glad when it's over, put it that way. But that doesn't mean to say I shan't get any meaning out of it.

I think it's very difficult – one could be cynical about this sort of thing and think, well, oh, it's only a ceremony, and some people are against it, and perhaps it's for TV and, you know, it's just a show.

I like to think it's a little more than just that …

Q. Charles was asked about his mother, the Queen.

A. She is just a marvellous person and wonderful mother. The Queen has a marvellous sense of humour and is terribly sensible and wise.

The TV interview received as much praise as his radio programme with Jack de Manio. The commentators began to talk of him as 'a natural'. Asked about the programmes later, Charles said: 'Yes, I did enjoy them. I wasn't really nervous, for some extraordinary reason. A lot depends on the interviewer, of course. Also I like acting and I enjoy imitating, which helps enormously when appearing in public.'

When Charles travelled to Caernarvon with his family in the royal train on the night of 30 June, he knew that he would need all his acting ability the next day as he appeared in his greatest public role so far. Even the Queen, with all her experience, was nervous and tense. The royal train was delayed for an hour at Crewe while a bomb disposal team dealt with a suspected bomb under a bridge outside Chester. It proved to be a hoax – two plasticine sticks attached to a ticking alarm clock.

Two days before a gelignite bomb had exploded at Cardiff Post Office, though fortunately no one was injured. Thousands of police had been in Caernarvon for some days, most of them in plain clothes, mixing with the people, listening and observing. Security at the Castle had been organized by a team of experts; it was impossible to move in or out without special passes and a search of belongings. Every inch of the building had been gone over not once, but many times. It was a rambling, ancient Norman castle with subterranean chambers and passages – a security man's nightmare. It was no laughing matter to recall Guy Fawkes and the Gunpowder Plot when Catholic conspirators had planted barrels of gunpowder in the cellars of the Houses of Parliament to blow up King James I, his ministers, and most of the establishment on 5 November 1605.

Arrangements for the ceremony had been initiated in September 1967, twenty-one months before, when a committee of fifty-three had started to sit. The man in charge was the late Duke of Norfolk, hereditary Earl Marshal (d. January 1975), who in the post-war years had proved his organizing ability and shrewdness with the media at the coronation of the Queen and, lately, at the state funeral of Sir Winston Churchill. This time, however, his duties were shared by a man of a younger generation, Lord Snowdon, Antony Armstrong-Jones before his marriage to Princess Margaret. The choice was excellent. As the 'Jones' part of his name showed, he was partly Welsh. His title of Snowdon linked him with the mountain and superb country which lies not far from Caernarvon. He had made a career as a photographer and was at the top of his profession before he married Margaret. He was a man of taste and imagination. His friends were drawn from a post-war generation of talented men and women working in the arts who could be expected to give a fresh touch to the investiture.

With the title of Constable, Snowdon was responsible for the Castle which was closed six months before the event. From the start TV experts were brought in. The ceremony would take place before a few thousand people, but the real audience would be up to four hundred million people who would see all or part on their television sets – many of them now equipped for colour. The distinguished audience, members of the royal family, ministers, members of the House of Lords and Commons, ambassadors, dignitaries, would, in fact, play parts in an historical pageant. The correct positioning of over eighty television cameras was of overriding importance. Fifty tons of turf had to be laid to give a uniform colour. The design of the dais, under which the ceremony would take place, the awning, the seating had to suit the TV cameras.

So far as the ceremony itself was concerned the Duke of Norfolk was determined it should conform to tradition. In fact, it was not much of a tradition. It dated back only to 1911 when Prince Edward (later King Edward VIII), the eldest son of King George V, was invested as Prince of Wales. The ceremony had lapsed for many centuries, but the Liberal Prime Minister, David Lloyd George, a Welshman, suggested to the King that its revival would help to strengthen the monarchy and the links of England with Wales. Lloyd George, who had started his political life as a left-wing firebrand, was changing with the possession of power. Also his parliamentary seat was Caernarvon.

The costume created for that Prince of Wales – white satin breeches, a mantle and surcoat of purple velvet edged with ermine – rankled with him for the rest of his life. Charles is, as he says, by temperament no rebel, but for this occasion his army uniform made no demands even on his sense of the ridiculous.

The royal train halted at a secret siding near the Menai Straits which separate Caernarvon from the beautiful island of Anglesey. They were given refreshments at the home of the Lord Lieutenant of the county, Sir Michael Duff.

In Caernarvon troops and police lined the streets of the attractive little town whose buildings had nearly all been painted at the expense of the local council. The Household Cavalry, brought up from London, waited to escort the open carriages of the procession. The special train carrying important guests arrived from London who then moved to their places in the Castle, but not without a careful scrutiny from the security men. The TV camera teams made last-minute adjustments; the commentators went through their briefing notes.

Two men blew themselves up with a faulty bomb thirty-five miles away. They had intended to blow up the local government offices. It was a very powerful bomb.

There were two minesweepers in the Straits; the harbour below the Castle had been sealed underwater; there were helicopters to survey the scene; there were closed-circuit television cameras to watch the crowds which were interspersed with carefully placed plain-clothes policemen. It was a tense time for the senior security officers. Some of them had seen service in Cyprus during the recent troubles and knew the well-nigh insuperable difficulties of dealing with well-trained terrorists. It was also a tense time for the royal family waiting for an ordeal they would have to face with smiles and waves.

Prince Charles set off for the Castle. As he drew near a 21-gun salute was fired and muffled the noise of an explosion not far away. The state trumpeters greeted him with a fanfare from the battlements. He went inside to wait in one of the towers for the summons from the Queen and watched television.

The Queen arrived amidst the clatter of the Household Cavalry. Then began the scenes of royal theatre. Lord Snowdon, as Constable, greeted her, bearing a huge 6lb foot-long key. He was wearing a uniform he had designed for himself as he had no military rank. It was a dark-green tunic and trousers with a belt of black silk. 'Madam', he said, 'I surrender the key of this castle into your Majesty's hand.' She replied, 'Sir Constable, I return the key of this castle into your keeping.'

The scene in the central courtyard was spectacular. On the ancient grey walls hung great banners recalling the history of Wales, with the fiery red dragon in pride of place. The emblem of the Prince of Wales, won at the Battle of Crécy in 1346 – the three ostrich feathers and the motto, 'Ich Dien' – gave six centuries of heraldic continuity. There were the Bards and the Chief Druid, in voluminous white robes, to recall the ancient religion of the Celts. There were splendid uniforms: the patchwork brilliance of the tabards of the heralds; the ermine-trimmed robes of the peers; the grey wigs and knee-breeches of municipal officers; interspersed among the dark

Charles and Anne watching the Barbary Apes on the Rock of Gibraltar when they went to meet their parents in the Mediterranean after their world-wide Coronation tour 1953/4.

The Queen visits Anne at Benenden School during the summer term of 1964.

'I could hardly see my hands for blisters after that.' Charles at Timbertop in Australia, 1965.

Edward begins to take notice of the world.

The first day at Cambridge. Lord Butler, Master of Trinity, greets a very special undergraduate in October 1967.

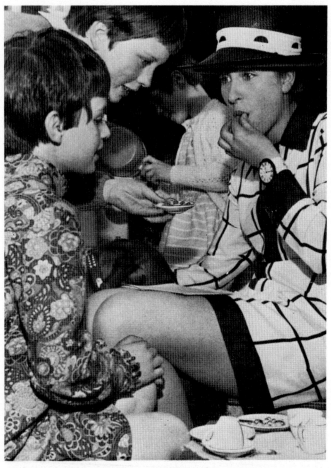

Anne appreciates a jelly baby when meeting the youngsters at a
children's home in 1969.

The spectacular scene in Caernarvon Castle on 1 July 1969, as Charles was invested as Prince of Wales by his mother. The battlements were manned by security men.

Chatting up the girls at Aberdare during a tour of Wales after the Investiture. He is discussing the badge worn by Ceri Jenkins, seventeen, a Queen's Guide.

Anne visits the 14/20th King's Hussars, of which she has been made Colonel-in-Chief, at their base in Paderborn, West Germany. She is wearing a colonel's tabs and a name tag, 'The Princess Anne'.

Christmas Day at Windsor Castle, 1969. Andrew commands a squad of family children which includes his brother Edward and his cousins, Viscount Linley, Lady Sarah Armstrong-Jones, the Earl of St Andrews, Lady Helen Windsor and James Ogilvy.

After church at Sandringham, 1969. Charles, Prince Philip, the Queen Mother, Princess Margaret, Andrew, Anne, Edward and the Queen.

Anne on Doublet at Burghley in September 1971, when she crowned a triumphant year by winning the Raleigh Trophy as Individual European Three-Day Event Champion.

In 1971 the readers of the *Daily Express* voted Anne Sportswoman of the Year and Jackie Stewart Sportsman of the Year. This was the *annus mirabilis* for Anne in her riding career.

Charles and Anne in Kenya during 1971. She is talking to the legendary President Kenyatta.

Edward, now seven, starts classes at Gibbs, a preparatory school in Kensington.

Charles had just made a parachute jump into the Channel as part of his RAF training in 1971.

formal morning-coats of the men the variegated colours of the women's summer dresses and hats. There were splendid choirs to sing 'The land of my fathers is dear to me', which expresses, as few national anthems do, the soul of a people.

Charles with a retinue of heralds and lords then appeared and came to the dais where the Queen was waiting. The Prince's insignia, carried by Welsh peers, was presented. The coronet, donated by the Goldsmiths' Company of the City of London, was new. It was a simple circlet decorated with crosses and fleur-de-lys, with arches carrying an orb and cross, made of gold and decorated with diamonds and emeralds. There was a silver-gilt sword, a rod made of Welsh gold, a golden ring of two dragons holding an amethyst, a mantle of purple trimmed with an ermine cape.

Charles knelt before his mother. Mr James Callaghan, then Home Secretary, read the Letters Patent creating her eldest son Prince of Wales and Earl of Chester. The insignia was piece by piece presented by the Queen to her son as Mr Callaghan read:

> And him our most dear son Charles Philip Arthur George as he has been accustomed We do enoble and invest with the said Principality and Earldom by girding him with a Sword by putting a coronet on his head and a Gold Ring on his finger and also by delivering a Gold Rod into his hand that he may preside there and may direct and defend those parts. To hold to him and his heirs Kings of the United Kingdom of Great Britain and Northern Ireland and of Our other Realms and Territories Heads of the Commonwealth for ever.

The Secretary of State for Wales, Mr George (later Lord) Thomas, then read the words in Welsh. Charles once more knelt before the Queen, placed his hands between hers, and swore the feudal oath: 'I, Charles Prince of Wales, do become your liege man of life and limb and of earthly worship, and faith and truth I will bear unto you to live and die against all manner of folks.'

The kiss of fealty, so often broken in the chequered history of medieval England, was given. The Queen sat in her throne chair and Charles sat on her right hand.

To a loyal address delivered in the two languages, Charles replied also in English and Welsh: 'It is indeed my firm intention to associate myself in word and deed with as much of the life of the Principality as possible. And what a Principality!'

The clergy blessed the ceremony, read from the Scriptures, and the choirs sang.

Then the Queen, wearing a Tudor-style hat and carrying a frilly parasol, went with her son, arrayed with his coronet and mantle, to present him to the people of Wales at the three gates – as it was said Edward I had presented his infant son in 1285. The link uniting seven hundred years of British history had been forged anew on 1 July 1969.

As the ceremony ended, the Queen, with Prince Charles sitting alongside in all his regalia, drove off to cheers, martial music, and the infinite relief of the police and security officers.

The royal yacht was anchored in the Menai Straits. Prince Charles, as Prince of Wales, gave a large dinner party and reception. There were parties all over the town and a ball at Glynllifon, formerly a great country-house.

On the next morning as the Palace press officers and the public relations advisers assembled their reports and analysed them, it was clear that the investiture had been a success beyond even the most optimistic expectations. Comments on the TV coverage (six hours by the BBC) and the journalist's eye-witness reports paid tribute to a magnificent royal spectacle and to Charles.

Even in Wales where the prospects, only a few months before, had seemed unpropitious, the reaction seemed astonishingly enthusiastic. Partially, perhaps, because the ceremony had renewed the traditions of Wales, the people and their language. Partially, as a tribute to a young man who had borne himself well. Partially, too, there was a touch of Celtic magic that had changed the hearts of many.

For Charles there was still a four-day tour of the Principality. It had its problems. On the day after the investiture an army truck exploded in the centre of Caernarvon killing a soldier who had been locked in after committing an offence against military discipline. Another bomb was discovered on a road near Bettws-y-Coed.

On Saturday 5 July, he greeted thousands of representatives of Welsh youth at Cardiff to end his tour. He sent a message to the people of Wales: 'My tour has been immensely moving in many ways and I have been deeply impressed by the evident trouble taken by so many people on and off the route.'

The investiture had been good for the monarchy, good for the country's morale, especially for Wales, and had given credit to Britain abroad. It had given a fine boost to Welsh tourism and the souvenir shops. When the profit and loss account had been counted up in terms of prestige and money, there was another factor to be considered: what had it done to Charles?

It had been an ordeal. There had been some risk and although it is fair enough to say that this was part of his job, it was still a strain for him. Charles said that afterwards he found himself waking up in the middle of the night waving his hand to imaginary crowds. In one way, this is an amusing, off-hand remark, but it also indicates some of the tension that he felt.

He had received abundant help from family, from officials, from public relations advisers, from innumerable sources, to ensure that the event was a success. In the final analysis, however, it was on his shoulders. To the world he had made it seem not a burden to be carried, but a joyous event to be shared.

7

Sportswoman of the Year

After the investiture, Charles had earned a break. With Anne, he flew off for a week's holiday to Malta. There was an agreeable reason for choosing Malta. Sybilla Dorman, then nineteen, was at Cambridge and Charles was somewhat taken with her. She was one of his guests on the *Britannia* after the investiture. And, as it happened, her father, Sir Maurice Dorman, was Governor-General of the island.

At the end of July Prince Charles and Princess Anne went with their parents to Torbay to review part of the Western Fleet during which the Queen was to present a new colour. There were receptions and ceremonies. Charles and Anne were each assigned visits to a number of warships. Anne was in great form, especially on HMS *Eastbourne* where she chatted with the crew, pretended to taste rum (she does not drink) and tasted a chip, telling the cook, 'You'll have to come to Buckingham Palace. We don't have any chips there.'

In early August the Queen organized a family treat – a cruise in the *Britannia* before the traditional Balmoral holiday. All four children, Charles, Anne, Andrew and Edward, embarked with their parents at Hull after the Queen had paid an official visit to the city. They sailed to the Shetland Islands and then crossed to Norway to spend a few days as guests of King Olav, who is a cousin.

It was a happy, informal visit among a people which treasure its links with Britain. They were greeted by King Olav at Bergen, visited Grieg's house at Troldhaugen, sailed with the accompanying Norwegian royal yacht, *Norge*, to Andalsnes and Molde, and finally had lunch with the Prime Minister,

Mr Per Borten, in his farmhouse outside Trondheim.

The Queen sailed back to Scotland with Andrew and Edward in *Britannia.* Prince Philip took Charles and Anne for a few more days' sailing in the Norwegian fjords in *Bloodhound*. Anne had her birthday on board. It was the last trip they would have on *Bloodhound*. Later in the year she was sold, apparently as an economy measure.

For Anne 1969 had been a good developing year in her riding. In addition to Purple Star, she had acquired a 16.2-hand thoroughbred, Royal Ocean, from Ireland. As it turned out, however, more important for her career, was the appearance on the scene of Doublet, who was owned by the Queen. He had been bred from an Argentine polo-pony mare and had been intended for Prince Philip's string, but grew too large. Anne and Doublet, a handsome chestnut, did not get along at all at first. But it was to be a great partnership.

In the Windsor Horse Trials on 30 April Anne rode Royal Ocean in Section D of the Novices Trials. There were twenty-seven starters and Anne won – eight points ahead of Mark Phillips on Great Ovation. By this time Anne was having to get used to criticism. It was said that she had had an unfair advantage at Windsor because she knew the course like the back of her hand and went round it every day. In fact, Anne had not ridden over any of the jumps for more than a year. But as a public competitor, she would have to take the rough with the smooth.

Considering that she now had official duties Anne's riding programme was phenomenal. She took part at Taplow, Basingstoke, Osberton, Eridge, Powderham Castle in Devon, Stoneleigh Abbey, Wylye, Stokechurch, Tweseldown and Chatsworth. In addition, she would try to get down to Alison Oliver's stables five or six times a week.

On 27 October she flew in a helicopter to a gas rig off the Norfolk coast. It was a production platform belonging to Amoco, one of the American oil companies which have been engaged in extracting gas and then oil from the North Sea. In a white boiler-suit and a safety-helmet Anne was given a view of one of the great technological marvels of the age – the deep-sea extraction of gas and oil which is changing the destiny of Great Britain.

The next day she flew to West Germany to visit the 14/20th King's Hussars as their new colonel-in-chief. They were stationed at Paderborn and on the way there the Germans gave her a civic welcome to which she replied in German much to their pleasure.

There was a regimental ball, a review of the tanks and a visit to the British Forces Educational School. Wearing khaki overalls she drove a Chieftain tank and fired a Sterling sub-machine gun from the hip. She attended a formal regimental dinner where the traditional toast of 'The Emperor' was drunk. 'The Emperor' in question was Napoleon and the toast is drunk from a silver chamber-pot captured by the Hussars from Napoleon's brother, King Joseph, when Wellington's army was driving the French from Spain. As the helicopter flew off at the end of the tour, the regimental band played, 'Oh, you beautiful doll!'

Prince Edward, now five, had started lessons at Buckingham Palace in a class of six under the new governess, Miss Lavinia Keppel. (Miss Peebles had died in October 1968). Miss Keppel was of the same family as Alice Keppel, the last and most lasting of Edward VII's mistresses. With Prince Edward in class were two cousins of the same age, Lady Sarah Armstrong-Jones and James Ogilvy.

Charles went back to Cambridge in the autumn. He still had a year to do before he took his finals in the summer of 1970. There had been so many interruptions to his studies that he knew he would have to work the harder. He did. 'You can't work as hard as he has', said his tutor, 'without interest, driving and staying-power.'

He carried on with his flying and graduated from the Chip-munk trainer to a twin-engined, six-seater Beagle Basset. He was playing squash, real tennis and polo, and getting out occasionally to the cinema and theatre. He also found time to help with a forty-five-minute TV documentary about the Welsh countryside which was shown on 5 May the following year.

In October he took time off to give an excellent speech before a large audience in the Albert Hall at a centenary concert in honour of the Indian leader, Mahatma Gandhi, who more than any one man had led India to independence. Charles appropriately spoke on the power of non-violence which had been at the centre of Gandhi's philosophy. Later in the month he was at a more hearty gathering. He opened the new clubhouse at Richmond of the London Welsh Rugby Club whose members may not be violent, but are certainly not devotees of passive resistance.

Charles's year was to end with another celebration – his twenty-first birthday party on 14 November at Buckingham Palace. There were over four hundred guests and Charles drew up the list with care. From his nanny onwards there were men and women who had helped him on his way or with whom he had formed a relationship – at Hill House, Cheam, Gordonstoun, Timbertop, Cambridge and in the RAF. There were people from Buckingham Palace, Windsor, Sandringham and Balmoral – high and low as they used to say. There were young cousins, male and female, from Germany. There was also Yehudi Menuhin, the master musician, whom Charles greatly admired. With him came a small orchestra to play court music of the eighteenth century – Haydn and Mozart – as a contrast to the modern dance music groups there. The sons and daughters of the court nobility were there in force. The champagne was of the best. The food delicious. After midnight the guests made their way to the garden terraces and watched a firework display that lit up the Palace, the lawns and the bare trees that stretched to Hyde Park. Charles had come of age.

He now came into full possession of the revenues of the Duchy of Cornwall. They total £220,000 a year, but as no income tax is paid a contribution of fifty per cent is made to the Treasury. This leaves Charles with a princely annual income of £110,000. (In 1977 the figure was about the same, in spite of the great inflation.)

Although the last guests did not leave until well into the morning hours, Charles was up betimes. He went to spend the week-end with one of the grandees of the country, the Duke of

Westminster, at his large estate in Chester. He was to shoot pheasant which were in season and among those to greet him was a ducal daughter, Lady Leonora Grosvenor, who was twenty.

With Charles coming of age, there were stories in the press speculating as to whether the Queen would decide on an early abdication in favour of her son. She would, in fact, be only forty-four in April 1970 and although she was facing the difficult years for a woman, she gave no sign of ill-health or of finding her position wearisome. The thinking behind the speculation probably had two reasons, apart from the fact that speculation about a possible abdication provides good material for newspapers and magazines. One reason was the fashionable cult of youth at the time. The second had some validity. Edward VII had been nearly sixty when he succeeded his mother, Queen Victoria, in 1901. During his best years his mother had consistently refused to allow him to do any responsible work. She might criticize him for his women, his gambling and his general life of pleasure, but would never allow him to participate in official business – even when the prime ministers and courtiers pleaded.

Charles took the early abdication matter up a few years later when he was asked about it:

No, I certainly don't think monarchs should retire, and be pensioned off, say, at sixty, as some professions and businesses stipulate. The nature of being a monarch is different. Take Queen Victoria. In her eighties, she was more loved, more known, more revered, and a more important part of the life of her country than she had ever been before. Looking at the monarchy as objectively as I can, I'd say retirement at a certain age is *not* a sensible idea.

In the same interview with Kenneth Harris, he went on:

The other point you made, if the monarch lives long and remains on the throne, isn't the heir-apparent kept out of things? Again, I'd say not. What matters is what *he* makes of things. There's plenty I can do. Especially when I am young. Precisely because I am *not* the sovereign, and therefore not so bound by the Constitution. I might be able to consider a wider range of possibilities of contributing. *And* I believe that if people see you are trying to make a contribution, and trying to be sensible, they'll give you all the support they can.

As 1970 started Charles, at twenty-one, and Anne, nineteen, were old enough to know and consider what was going on in the world, and to be able to assess what they could do to help Britain and the Commonwealth. They had passed their youth in years, which though at times internationally dangerous, had seen a quite remarkable degree of prosperity in Britain, in the industrialized countries generally, and even an improvement in the poor countries of the world.

The climate was now changing. Inflation was beginning to get out of hand. In banking and commercial circles there was unease and a growing lack of confidence in the future. In November 1968 Harold Wilson, the Prime Minister, and his Chancellor, James Callaghan, had been forced to devalue sterling after a three-year battle to preserve its value. It brought higher prices, cuts in government expenditure, an inevitable increase in unemployment. By the end of that year of 1968 there had been heavy sales of sterling and a mood of panic had gripped the City of London. In one day in December there were rumours that the Prime Minister was going to resign, that there was to be a coalition government and that the Queen was abdicating.

So far as the royal family was concerned, the changed economic climate had already made an impact. At the end of 1969 Prince Philip informed the American public in a TV programme that the royal family was 'going into the red'. He added, 'if nothing happens we shall have to – I don't know, we may have to move into smaller premises, who knows? We've closed down – well, for instance, we had a small yacht (*Bloodhound*) which we've had to sell, and I shall probably have to give up polo fairly soon, things like that.'

His outburst caused an uproar back in Britain. He had, it seemed, chosen an American platform to get action from the

British government, which happened to be Labour, but was approaching the end of its term and would soon be calling a general election.

Harold Wilson explained to the House of Commons that talks about the official royal income (which had been fixed, according to tradition, at the beginning of the reign) had been going on for some time between the Treasury and Palace officials. He said that his government had told the Palace that the matter would be dealt with by the next government. He added that there was adequate machinery to deal with any emergencies that might arise. There were no emergencies.

When the Conservatives won the following election in June 1970, a select committee was set up to examine the royal finances and the country's contribution was doubled. It has since been regularly reviewed and has been made virtually inflation-proof, a privilege not enjoyed by the vast majority of the Queen's subjects who have seen their standards of living heavily reduced. It has been a very considerable privilege indeed.

The Commonwealth was the other great subject. In the years when Charles and Anne had been growing up the British Empire had died, but, in a quite remarkable and unexpected way, was transformed into a Commonwealth that showed signs of surviving. For the Queen, this had been her greatest challenge and the field in which she felt that she could make a positive contribution. She had travelled tirelessly; she had created personal links throughout the world and by her personality and increasing experience helped to strengthen a Commonwealth which was at times so unsure of itself that it might have disintegrated.

For Charles decisions were taken about his career after Cambridge. It was expected of him that he should spend some time with the services. He appreciated this and was quite amenable now that he had had his way and gone first to Cambridge. It was announced that in the spring of the following year, 1971, he would go to RAF Cranwell and take a four months' advanced flying course. He was looking forward to this. He enjoyed flying, he was proving a good pilot, and would go to

Cranwell with many more hours' flying experience than most of his contemporaries. Then he was to go to the Royal Naval College at Dartmouth for a crash course and spend at least three years in the navy. It seemed as if, after the promise he had shown already in public life, he was to be hidden for years behind the armour plating of warships. It was not to turn out quite like that, however. Charles was now having a say in the way his life was organized.

The Queen had decided that now that Charles was twenty-one and Anne nineteen, it was the right time to take them with her on the major Commonwealth tours which she and Prince Philip were making that year. It would be a family introduction before Charles and Anne made their own visits in the future.

In April the family started a two months' tour of Australia, New Zealand and the Pacific islands, Fiji and Tonga. Aircraft and the royal yacht were used as transport and enabled a heavy programme to be carried out. The Queen used the 'walk-about' technique for the first time.

The tour fulfilled its purpose. The Australians and New Zealanders were able to see their royalty as a family with two promising youngsters growing up to represent a new generation. The message about Anne and horses had been taken. She had mounts in New Zealand and stayed two days at a private property in Australia, Talbarea Station at Cunnamulla, where she had plenty of riding. But Charles was the success. The Australians knew how much he had enjoyed his two terms at Timbertop and greeted him as a son who had been absent for a time. In New Zealand, too, Charles struck just the right note. He seemed almost more at home in the Antipodes than he was in Britain. It is, he has said, the lack of pretention and the sincerity in those countries which makes him feel he is a worthwhile person in his own right.

Charles went back to Cambridge and sat for his finals in history. He passed with a creditable second-class degree – more than creditable if all his official duties are taken into account. It was time to pack his books at Cambridge and put the under-graduate's gown away. It had been the first year there that had mattered to Charles. It had been the time of freedom, talk, amateur dramatics, girlfriends, sport and hilarious dining and wining with his contemporaries. It had been his choice to go to university. He had made a success of it, both at Cambridge and Aberystwyth. He had enjoyed it all and made friends, some of whom would remain staunch friends.

In July Charles and Anne went with their parents to Canada. It was arranged that the young people should go off on their own for a time and meet some of their contemporaries. At Manitoba University in Winnipeg Charles said bluntly: 'I want to change the old image of remote royalty. I want people to meet me and realize I'm just a normal sort of person and not so very different from anyone else.' Anne exercised her own form of bluntness. When one of the students said he was studying political science, she commented: 'More politicians should study that because they don't ever seem to learn from the mistakes of their predecessors.'

At the end of the Canadian tour Charles and Anne were invited by President Nixon and his wife to spend a few days with them at the White House in Washington. It was no doubt a kindly meant gesture with only a minimal political implication. But it would have been just as well if it had never happened. For Anne it was a disaster. American journalists may not be more aggressive than their fellows in Britain and Europe, but they have no special sense of reticence when it comes to dealing with royalty, especially when they are a young prince and princess, descendants of King George III of black memory in Washington.

Charles was able to cope; perhaps his Australian experience helped. Anne lost her temper on several occasions when she was asked personal questions, and was more than brusque in reply. In consequence she received a bad press in America which took years to live down. Charles's problems were inside the White House. Mr Nixon's daughter, Tricia, had been an honoured guest at the investiture at Caernarvon the previous year. But he later told an American hostess in an unguarded moment at a party, 'I didn't much like it when Mr Nixon and his wife started matching me up with their elder daughter.

Which one is she? Tricia, isn't that right? I found her artificial and plastic.'

Discussion about whom Charles would, should or could marry has been a matter for endless speculation. Charles, probably after discussion with his parents, has worked out an answer to the question which is sensible, but, inevitably, sounds cold and calculating. In the TV programme before the investiture he said on this subject:

This is awfully difficult because you have got to remember that when you marry in my position, you are going to marry somebody who perhaps one day is going to be Queen. You have got to choose somebody very carefully, I think, who could fulfil this particular role and it has got to be somebody pretty special. The one advantage about marrying a princess, for instance, or somebody from a royal family, is that they tend to know what happens.

The only trouble is that I often feel that I would like to marry somebody English, or, perhaps, Welsh ... well, British anyway.

In fact, it was not the only trouble Charles would have when the question of marriage became important. Under an Act of 1689, establishing the Protestant succession, Charles could not marry a Roman Catholic. He also could not marry without the approval of his mother under the terms of the Royal Marriage Act of 1772 which George III had caused to be passed when two of his sons had made marriages he did not approve of.

The amateur match-makers had already noticed that there was a notable lack of princesses of the right age from the reigning Protestant royal families of Europe – the Dutch, Danish, Norwegian and Swedish houses. Protestant German princesses there were, but they bore titles that still brought disagreeable memories to the British.

Anne's riding career had reached a stage when it had to be taken seriously by her family. She was working at it with almost obsessive devotion and word was spreading from the 'horsey' circles to Fleet Street that Anne was determined to reach the top.

She said: 'It's the one thing that the world can see I can do well that's got *nothing* whatever to do with my position, or money, or anything else. If I'm good at it, I'm good at it – and not because I'm Princess Anne.'

Her mother saw no harm in her daughter pressing on doing what she wanted. She loved horses herself and, anyway, it provided an outlet for Anne's energies and interest – and she had not been the happiest of girls in her teens. Prince Philip, fond as he was of his daughter, was not so enthusiastic about her entering the highly competitive and public world of top-class horsemanship. He realized Anne would have to face criticism as well as praise.

He had probably envisaged for his daughter a career in some form of public service such as the care of deprived or sick children here and in the Commonwealth. He is a serious-minded man and saw for Anne a fulfilment, which could last a lifetime, in some form of humanitarian service. It would be good for her; it would also be good for the monarchy.

But Anne was obstinate and had her own way. Her official duties were little more than interruptions in her life at Alison Oliver's establishment at Brookfield: there were the loose-boxes with room for nearly thirty horses; there was the indoor school to study and practise the intricate art of dressage; there was the paddock with the cross-country fences. Anne would drive down to arrive around 8.30 am, put in two or three hours, drive back to London, if necessary, to fulfil a function and then drive down again in the evening, when the daylight was good, for another hour or two. It was dedication. In addition there were the succession of competitive public trials all over the country where Anne was beginning to make her mark.

Alison Oliver's part in the programme was vital. She not only gave Anne her own knowledge and skill, she looked after Anne's horses far beyond the call of duty to ensure they were as near perfection as possible when she rode them.

The first great hurdle was to qualify for the Badminton Three-Day Event in April 1971. Badminton is to horse trials what Lord's is to cricket, Wimbledon to tennis and Henley to rowing. Yet curiously, it is a post-war development in England.

In Europe equestrianism had always flourished as a combination of art, courage and endurance. The Duke of Beaufort, Master of the Queen's Horse – a largely ceremonial post – was a great foxhunter. In the season he considered a day when he was not out, a day lost. He was also interested in equesrianism, and after the war opened up his estate at Badminton, bordering the Cotswolds, for an annual event which would be of a class equal to that of any country. He hoped it would act as a spur to the young men and women to excel and gradually put Britain into the top Olympic class.

At Badminton every spring the horse-boxes disgorge their beautiful animals; the shooting-brakes disgorge their men and women, not always beautiful, but certainly groomed for the occasion in tweeds, heavy raincoats, caps, bowlers and head-scarves. The Queen, the Queen Mother and Princess Margaret are nearly always there and greatly increase the prestige of the occasion.

Badminton is centred on the three-day event and only horses and riders who have achieved some measure of success can be entered. It is a daunting test of horsemanship.

The first day is given over to dressage, a complicated art in which Europeans had excelled, but which the British had neglected. It is a test, short in time, but nerve-racking in intensity. There must be a complete *rapport* between horse and rider as the various paces are exhibited. It is not so much a matter of the rider giving the horse orders, as the expression of complete identity between rider and horse. It was this aspect of horsemanship which had given Anne so much trouble.

The second day is devoted to speed and endurance. There is a long ride through tracks and paths, then a steeplechase, but the real test is still to come – the cross-country. For 1971 the course was longer than the previous year and consisted of thirty-one obstacles. There were tree-trunks, parallel bars, hedges, walls, open water, ditches and rails.

The third day is for show-jumping, known to millions now through television. In 1971 Badminton had an eleven-fence course, including three doubles and an open water.

Altogether, the Badminton Three-Day Event could be considered one of the toughest equestrian competitions in the world. Anne and Doublet did finally qualify to take part.

They would be competing against the top-class – Mary Gordon-Watson and Cornishman, holders of the Individual World and European Champion titles; Lorna Sutherland and Peer Gynt; Mark Phillips and Great Ovation; Debbie West and Baccarat; Hazel Booth and Mary Poppins. Richard Meade, one of Britain's most experienced riders, would also be there. These young men and women were already an integral part of Anne's world. From them she drew her friends.

In addition Badminton had drawn competitors from Ireland, Holland, Switzerland and Sweden. It was very much an international event by now.

The Queen stays with the Duke of Beaufort at Badminton House when she visits the Horse Trials. When it was known Anne would be competing the royal family party grew. Apart from the Queen there were Prince Philip, the Queen Mother, Prince Charles, Prince Andrew and Prince Edward.

In horsey circles there was some scepticism whether Anne would not be out of her class; it was doubted whether she would get round. The comments reached Fleet Street where it was now becoming clear that Badminton would be a big news story, whatever happened. The specialist writers, columnists, reporters and photographers were mobilized. The French magazines sent over a picked team of their toughest and ablest.

Lieutenant Colonel Frank Weldon, director of the trials, was asked to comment and said: 'She is a very determined young woman and determination is really the beginning and the end of the sport.'

At the end of March, after it had been announced she would ride at Badminton, she had a fall at the Crookham Horse Trials. It was remembered that she had had a number of falls in public and had broken her nose riding a pony whilst at school.

Alison Oliver said of her pupil: 'She is so mad keen that she never tires of practice, practice and more practice.' She added: 'Some experts say she is a stylish rider, but I think workmanlike is a better description. She has determination plus a load of guts.'

The day arrived. On Friday 22 April it was dressage. Anne ended in the lead, a splendid start. On the Saturday there was torrential rain turning the ground into a sea of mud. Anne had no trouble with the roads, tracks and steeplechase. Then came the daunting cross-country with forty-eight starters. She had a first-class round with no jumping penalties. At the end of the second day she was in fourth place. On the Sunday, the third day, she went round the course with only one mistake.

Her final place was fifth out of forty-eight, a really first-class performance. Anne was satisfied. Alison Oliver justified. Anne's family were proud. The outright winner was, as it happened, Mark Phillips.

The press enthused. So did radio and television. The photographers had no disasters to record, only splendid riding. The British respect success in sport, whatever the sport. Anne's prowess became a talking-point. 'My God, the girl's got guts – and skill.'

Already horizons were widening for Anne. There was the European Three-Day Event Championship to be held at Burghley in September. Would she be chosen? There were commentators pointing out that the Olympic Games would be held in Munich in the following year, 1972, and that Badminton and Burghley would play their part in deciding who represented Britain in the equestrian team. Was Anne getting near to being considered?

These were dazzling prospects for Anne. She desperately wanted to be in the Olympic team, but she tried hard not to hope too much. It was a long time ahead, and Anne was aware that it is a disadvantage to be a girl when there are high officials in the eventing world with a professed preference for a male team – and also that it was probably another disadvantage to be a princess.

A few weeks after Badminton (Doublet had been given by the Queen as a present to Anne for her performance there) Anne was given the chance to ride at Burghley as an individual, not as part of the official short-list of eight.

Anne could press on with her training with the agreeable feeling that now she was surrounded by approval. In July, however, she had to go into hospital for an abdominal operation and although she is strong it put her back for a few weeks. Burghley was becoming so important to her that her twenty-first birthday on 15 August seemed almost incidental. She spent it quietly with her family at the Queen Mother's holiday home, the Castle of Mey, near Thurso, on the north-east tip of Scotland. Being twenty-one is important in itself, but for Anne it had an added, welcome financial aspect. She started to draw £15,000 a year from the Civil List.

The prospect of Burghley, which started on 2 September, took its toll of Anne's nervous strength. She admitted afterwards that she had three sleepless nights before the event. But, against stiff competition, she won. The crowd cheered. The photographers were insatiable. The Queen was there to hand her the Raleigh Trophy as Individual European Three-Day Event Champion.

Public acclaim reached new heights. She was chosen Sports' Personality of the Year by the votes of BBC viewers; Sportswoman of the Year by the Sportswriters' Association; Sportswoman of the Year by the readers of the *Daily Express*. 'I am delighted to have been chosen for this honour', she told the newspaper, 'and am looking forward very much to Friday's presentation lunch.'

Hopes of her being chosen for the Munich Olympics were raised in the press to confident expectation. It had been a great year for Anne. It was her first year of fame in her chosen career. But that first year was never to be matched again.

What Prince Philip had feared already started to happen before the end of the year.

Harvey Smith, one of the great names in the British horse world, said of Anne at a public dinner: 'In her own class she is very good, but that is nowhere near Olympic standards. It would be like throwing our best heavyweight boxer into the ring with Cassius Clay. It is too soon and the gap's too big.'

He was criticized for his remarks, but it was not long before Lieutenant Colonel Weldon of Badminton remarked that Anne did not have 'a cat in hell's chance of going to Munich as a member of Britain's Olympic team.'

Anne had joined the competitive world of sport and asked to be judged on her merits. She was finding out the hard way that that was exactly what would happen.

In Anne's own way she had proved her point in 1971. Two years earlier Charles had been the centre of the news when he was being invested as Prince of Wales – because he was the eldest son of the monarch. Anne could say to herself that she was Sportswoman of the Year and all the rest because of her own efforts, courage and determination.

Whatever happened in the future, nobody could take that achievement away from her.

Anne had also made her TV debut in 1971. In April the BBC showed her in the children's programme *Blue Peter* which had been made when she visited Kenya earlier with Charles for a two-week tour. It was called *Royal Safari* and showed her, often on horseback, touring the magnificent game parks and seeing for herself some of the activities of the Save the Children Fund of which she had been appointed the British president. With the capable BBC interviewer, Val Singleton, Anne visited the Starahe Boys' Centre, rode through a coffee plantation, was filmed in a riding session, and made knowledgeable comments in her brusque style.

In the same programme she was asked about clothes and remarked sharply: 'It is always a total mystery to me why I am described as a fashion leader. Clothes are part of the job – if you can call it a job.' For Anne, however, this was a fairly mild remark. She had had for some years a biting tongue. Unfortunately, her parents were unable to soften it.

Before the showing of the TV film Anne was involved in her first public motoring accident. She drove into a mini-cab in the Brompton Road, Knightsbridge. She was driving her Reliant Scimitar with her detective alongside. It was not serious; the detective did all he could to smooth over the affair, but it was Anne's fault.

Later Anne went with her father as representatives of the Queen at the sumptuous celebrations at Persopolis in Iran of the 2,500th anniversary of its history. The Shah, rich with oil revenues from the fields discovered by the British, wished to recall to distinguished representatives of the world the splendour and continuity of Iranian history. In the ruins of Persopolis a splendid temporary town was established with every luxury that money could command.

For Anne opportunities to ride were made available on an imperial scale. There are splendid stables at Farahabad outside Teheran, including a small, delightful palace for the Shah's relaxation. Anne rode one of the magnificent stallions, Belderchine, and saw some of the wild beauty of the imperial hunting reserve. It was an enviable experience. The Shah gave her as a gift a beautiful bay colt, Atesh, meaning 'Fire'.

Charles completed his Cranwell advanced flying course with great *élan* and his report described him as 'above the average'. He had clocked up so many hours flying before he went that he was able to take on the jets with a certain amount of confidence, although he showed himself a meticulous trainee who listened and did not try to fool around. In this field he shows a competitive spirit and likes to be as good as anyone. He describes flying, so far as he is concerned, as 'a mixture between fear and supreme enjoyment'.

After getting his wings at the beginning of August Charles went up to Balmoral to join the family. Although he was soon to join the navy, he managed to spend two days with his regiment, the Royal Regiment of Wales, at Osnabrück in West Germany. In the mess, as a relatively new officer, although an exalted colonel-in-chief, he went through the ritual of eating a raw leek and sang a song. It was a Goon Song.

Charles was determined not to be just a figurehead in the regiment. He arranged to have monthly reports sent to him. Whenever they have done a stint in Northern Ireland he has wanted to be kept informed about the wounded, the widows and the families. When a wounded man is convalescing he gets at least one bottle of Scotch from the colonel-in-chief.

During his visit he asked various soldiers how they were getting on and found that one of their troubles was making themselves understood by the German girls. Charles re-marked:

> I said something ought to be done about *that*, so I sug-gested I should supply them with a special phrase-book to assist them in their amorous exploits, and coming back in the aircraft I drew up a list of words and phrases which I thought might be useful. My secretary, who spoke very good German, translated them, and I sent them back a few days later a light-hearted phrase-book. They seemed pleased. Not because they really needed the German, but because I kept my promise after I had addressed the battalion.

In fact, Charles speaks good German, not as fluently as his father, Prince Philip, who is almost bi-lingual. The Palace plays down this talent of both father and son because even now there is some prejudice and it is not wished to emphasize the German links of the royal family.

Before he joined the Royal Navy at Dartmouth instructions were given that on formal occasions all officers, including admirals, were to bow on meeting him and their wives were to curtsey. The address was, 'Your Royal Highness'. In his workaday life, however, Charles was given and accepted orders like any other junior officer and he did his best to make the social life as informal as possible. At Dartmouth he used to go out with his fellows and take a drink in the local pubs and established a good relationship.

Immediately after the course he went to sea as an acting sub-lieutenant in the guided missile destroyer, *Norfolk*, which was going on a five weeks' exercise in the Mediterranean.

Charles was joining a navy changed very much even from the days of his father. Ludovic Kennedy, a highly knowledgeable writer on naval affairs, says:

> First the men. It is no exaggeration to say that the morale of the navy, traditionally always high, has probably never been higher. Relations between officers and men, too, are much more relaxed and informal. Today's navy is probably

the nearest we have yet got to a classless society: one officer in three was once a rating himself: he shares with the ratings a sort of professional middle ground.

With the advance of technology, nearly every officer is what would have been described in the wartime navy as a 'boffin' — a scientist. Degrees and further degrees are part of the background of many in the wardroom. This was to be part of Charles's problem in the navy. 'The trouble is', Charles said later, 'people expect one to be a genius.'

Prince Edward, now seven, became a day-boy at Gibbs, a preparatory school in Kensington. With him was Princess Alexandra's son, James Ogilvy. Prince Andrew, who was eleven this year, came into the news in a way that foreshadowed his somewhat aggressive attitude to life. He was one of a party of boys who were brought up to London from their fashionable prep-school, Heatherdown at Ascot, to visit the Natural History Museum at South Kensington. They encountered boys from another school. Before the masters could separate them, there was a scuffle which disturbed the tranquil galleries.

Heatherdown had more serious problems. It was a time of IRA kidnap threats and security had to be increased as a precautionary measure for, apart from Prince Andrew, a son of the Duke of Kent, the Earl of St Andrew, was also at the school.

It was a sign of the times.

8

Wedding Splendour

Doublet, the horse that had brought Anne her triumphs in 1971, had bruised a tendon during the Burghley competition. At the time it did not seem of much importance. He was given three months' rest and then Alison Oliver worked out a programme of training to prepare Anne and the horse for the Badminton Trials in April 1972. Whatever cold water may have been thrown on the ambition, Anne, with Alison Oliver's encouragement, was hoping that a further success at Badminton would give her a chance of being chosen for that year's Olympics in Munich. Anne's sights were firmly fixed on it.

In February she went with the Queen and Prince Philip on a magnificent tour of the Far East. They saw the colour and beauty of Thailand, Malaysia, Singapore, Brunei, Malacca, Mauritius and the Seychelles. Everywhere there was smiling hospitality and spectacular functions. But part of Anne's mind was back at Brookfield, thinking about her horses, especially Doublet.

As soon as she returned she was back at the stables. By the beginning of April Doublet was in perfect shape. At the end of March Anne took him to compete at Crookham. The dressage test was excellent; they had a clear run in the show-jumping; on the cross-country Anne did not press him hard, but they kept eighth place overall. But the damaged tendon was a worry. Alison Oliver decided to give Doublet a hard gallop on Newbury Downs to see what would happen under the degree of strain likely to be encountered at Badminton. The worst happened; there was a swelling and it did not go down. Doublet would have to be withdrawn. It was the end of Anne's Olympic hopes for 1972.

It was a terrible disappointment and she felt it bitterly. She went, however, as a spectator to Badminton and watched with a certain wistfulness the exploits of the competitors, many of them her friends and rivals. She got over her disappointment finally. But it was a slow process.

In fact, the British Equestrian Team, of which Mark Phillips was a member, won gold medals at Munich. Anne was there as a spectator, but these were the Games that were marred by the Palestinian Arab terrorists' attack on the Israeli athletes of whom eleven were killed in the subsequent shootings.

After his relationship at Cambridge with the glamorous Lucia Santa Cruz, Charles had had various casual friendships with girls who were not much more than 'dates'. This year, however, the quite remarkable Georgiana Russell came into his life. She is the daughter of Sir John Wriothesley Russell, a kinsman of the Duke of Bedford, and his wife Aliki, who was a Greek beauty queen. Sir John was a highly successful, extrovert and unconventional ambassador in Brazil (he was there when the Queen paid her state visit in 1968) and then in Madrid. Everywhere Georgiana, stunningly beautiful and highly intelligent, had won acclaim. A Brazilian newspaper wrote of her as 'the living expression of all that is young and free in Britain today'. She speaks seven languages, plays the piano, harp and guitar, and is quite enchanting. Before she left Brazil she was voted one of the country's eleven best-dressed women and an editorial thanked the Queen for sending Georgiana.

In Spain she became the idol of Madrid. In 1971 she came to London to work for *Vogue*. She met Charles and he was fascinated. He was spending much of this year ashore at Portsmouth and Chatham and he took every opportunity to take Georgiana out in London and arrange weekends where they would be together. She went to Windsor to see him play polo in April: she was a guest at Sandringham and Balmoral.

The romance lasted until the end of the year. Georgiana

said: 'If I say anything, I will get stink from my parents. I really will.'

At the end of the year she left England to work in Paris. She commented later, rather sadly: 'I don't think I was ever a favourite in the marriage stakes.'

Prince Charles did a sub-lieutenant's course at the shore-based HMS *Excellent* at Portsmouth. His special sense of humour was developing in the navy. During the course he became aware that two Australians and a New Zealander were indulging in a bit of fun at his expense. At the dinner which marked the end of the course he remarked on this and said, 'Little did they know that all I had to do was blow a whistle.' He promptly blew a whistle. In marched three of his fellow-officers on the course wearing the uniform of the Beefeaters who guard the Tower of London, traditional prison of traitors. It all went down very well. He passed the course and was posted to the frigate *Minerva*.

Charles was called away to attend the funeral at Windsor of his great-uncle, the Duke of Windsor who had died in Paris at the age of nearly seventy-eight on 28 May. The Duke, who had reigned less than a year as King Edward VIII, had abdicated on 10 December 1936 to marry an American, Mrs Wallis Simpson, who had been twice divorced. The Governments of Britain and the Dominions had already informed him that if he was determined to marry her, he would have to renounce the throne. For Charles the history of the Duke was of particular significance. He had been the last Prince of Wales before him and in the twenties and thirties had been the idol of the nation. His impatience with tradition, his desire to bring the monarchy closer to the people, had won him popularity, but his final actions as king had endangered the institution. Charles could regard him very much as an awful warning.

Charles had shortly after to attend another family funeral. The young Prince William of Gloucester, son and heir of the Duke of Gloucester, the Queen's uncle, was killed when a small aircraft he was piloting crashed at a rally.

Charles found time to appear in an ITV programme on the world of sport and talked about polo at which he was now a good player. Shortly afterwards he captained a Young England team against the visiting Young Americans.

Anne had another disappointment in her riding career at Burghley in the autumn. She was riding Columbus, a large dapple-grey which belonged to the Queen and had for some time, with another grey, Collingwood, formed part of Anne's training stable. She had to retire from the competition.

However, this autumn Anne's friendship with Mark Phillips became closer and they started to see more of each other on their own. Mark Phillips was to boast later that 'the press would be surprised how often we have been out to dinner and they haven't noticed it'.

In October Charles spent two days with his regiment, the Royal Regiment of Wales, who were doing a spell of duty in the West sector of Berlin. It is a slightly claustrophobic posting, surrounded by East German territory and facing the Berlin Wall. Charles thought it would be a good idea to go and see them. No doubt he was able to see if his German phrasebook had won results!

Charles and Anne had a joint task this autumn. On 20 November, their mother and father were celebrating their silver wedding anniversary. There was public celebration – a school holiday, a service in Westminster Abbey, where they had been married, a drive through London and a grand lunch at Guildhall given by the Lord Mayor and the City of London.

There was also to be a big family dinner party. Charles and Anne arranged the musical entertainment and asked Sir John Betjeman, whose verse Charles so much admires, to produce some lines for the printed programme. Betjeman came up with:

> Queen of the open air, the rock and heather,
> Twenty-five years ago who would have known
> You and your sailor prince would build together
> Such family affection for the throne.
> For all your humour, calm and selfless living
> Your subjects join me in today's thanksgiving.

Not exactly Betjeman at his best, but it went down well at the festive board.

It was probably no more than the fact that the Queen and Prince Philip were celebrating their silver wedding that prompted another wave of rumour that the Queen would make way for her son. This time the year mentioned was 1977, when the Queen would have reigned twenty-five years.

In January 1973 it was announced that Charles would be sailing the following month in the frigate *Minerva* for a six months' tour of duty in the West Indies. Before he left he took his love of Cambridge days, Lucia Santa Cruz, to a symphony concert in London. It was an agreeable consolation as Georgiana had gone abroad. The two women had certain similarities, apart from beauty and intelligence. They were exotics. Neither of them represented the typical aristocratic English girl.

In January, while the royal family were spending their Christmas holidays at Sandringham, Mark Phillips was invited to stay. When he left to rejoin his regiment in Germany Anne drove him to Harwich and gave him a chaste kiss on the cheek. This was enough for Fleet Street to get busy. At this time Anne and Mark Phillips began to show increasing impatience with the press whose representatives were, under the circumstances, only doing their job.

By the time Charles sailed for the West Indies in February, Fleet Street had enough information, it felt, to be confident that Anne and Mark Phillips were to become engaged. By March the papers were full of it.

Each denied any romance. Mark Phillips said: 'Princess Anne and I are just good friends with a common interest and great love of horses.' Anne's parents told the Buckingham Palace press office to circulate a discreet denial of any romance to the editors of Fleet Street.

Fleet Street was not satisfied with the denial. When she made an appearance at the Amberley horse show near Cirencester she was surrounded by a crowd of photographers. She lost her temper and said, amongst other things, 'I don't know why I am being subjected to this nonsensical treatment. This is what raises my blood pressure. I'm just sitting here doing nothing.'

The halcyon days of 1971 when Anne had been the darling of Fleet Street had gone. Anne had always had a blistering tongue on occasions. Now it was getting worse and becoming almost savage. It was not just the marriage rumours; she felt the photographers were interfering with her riding career, upsetting her horse at critical moments, and were only happy when they could take a picture of her falling. Her reactions may also have been partially due to the frustrations and lack of success she had enjoyed since the *annus mirabilis* of 1971.

A Buckingham Palace spokesman, commenting on the Amberley troubles, said: 'The trouble with all this fuss is that it upsets the horses and also upsets the other competitors. Everyone has said there is no romance and that's that.'

In April both Anne and Mark Phillips were at Badminton. Anne did creditably, finishing eighth on a new horse, Goodwill. She was on the short-list to attend the European Championships in September which this year were being held at Kiev in Soviet Russia. It was a fact of interest to the experts that the British short-list was composed entirely of women.

Although Anne had been chosen on her merits, there had been discussions first in the royal family and then with ministers before the decision to participate was made. For no member of the royal family had set foot in Russia since the 1917 Revolution. The British royal family had been connected by blood to the Tsar and his family who had been murdered during their imprisonment. However, British relations with Russia were now reasonably amiable. The Queen had entertained Soviet leaders in London. The Conservative Government, led by Mr Edward Heath, felt that the visit might well do good and the Russians were pleased to welcome Anne and Prince Philip, who would be going as President of the International Equestrian Federation. Prince Philip, always eager for new experiences, wanted to go and it was arranged he should have two days in Moscow.

Then, just like that, it was announced on 29 May that Princess Anne and Lieutenant Mark Phillips were engaged and that the wedding would be in Westminster Abbey on 14 November, which would be Charles's twenty-fifth birthday.

Fleet Street, loyal as ever on such occasions, gave the news a great welcome, but there were some rueful comments on the flat denial of March. As Charles remarked later to Stuart Kuttner of the *Evening Standard* when discussing his own life: 'But as you know only too well, the problem as a result of my sister announcing her engagement, having said only a few months previously that there was no truth in the rumours, is that the press, I know, will never ever again believe it if you say there is no truth and we're just good friends.'

Anne explained on television: 'People don't believe when we say that in March we had no intention of getting married. In fact it is absolutely true and it was only after Badminton (April) ... that it seemed like a good idea.'

Anne's courtship had had its setbacks. 'He kept telling me', she said, 'he was a confirmed bachelor and I thought at least one knows where one stands. I mean, I wasn't thinking about it.'

Anne was asked if she had been free to marry the man of her choice. She replied: 'It has never been mentioned. I don't think there had been any question of it so far as the family was concerned.' This was somewhat disingenuous of Anne. The man she was to marry would have had to pass the test of her family as being eligible and the governments of Great Britain and some senior Commonwealth countries would have had to give their approval.

Mark Phillips was born in September 1948 and so was two years older than Anne. On his father's side the family had in the nineteenth century worked its way up. In one generation a miner, in the next a mining engineer. His mother's family, Tiarks, had been pewterers at Jever in Germany in the eighteenth century and then they became Lutheran clergymen. Johann Gerhard Tiarks became chaplain to Queen Victoria's mother, the Duchess of Kent. The Duchess, a Coburg, had been left a widow with two children by the Prince of Leiningen before she married the Duke of Kent. Tiarks settled in England and his descendants found their place mainly in the professions or the army. Mark's mother was the daughter of a brigadier who was an aide-de-camp to King George VI.

Mark's father, Peter Phillips, had served in the army, reached the rank of major and then gone into business becoming a director of Wall's, one of the best-known food firms in the country. He and his wife lived in a sixteenth-century manor house and also farmed. In the terms of today they would rank very much as a country family. Trade is no longer a handicap, but a welcome source of income for the gentry.

At Marlborough Mark was known as a modest, hard-working, amiable boy. He intended to go into the army like his father. His academic record was not good enough to win him a place at Sandhurst (the army picks and chooses nowadays). Not to be deterred, he joined the ranks of the Royal Green-jackets and won a place in an officers' training academy. He passed out and got a commission in the Queen's Dragoon Guards in which his father had served.

Charles had been alerted in the West Indies of his sister's impending engagement and flew back for a short holiday on 26 May so that he could join in the engagement party which was held in the seclusion of a house on the Balmoral estate.

Charles had not let his naval duties neglect his other interests and his office at Buckingham Palace run by David Checketts kept him in touch. He sent a regular report of his activities to his regiment. 'I started doing this', he remarked, 'because I thought if it interests *me* to read about what's going on with *them*, it might interest *them* to read about what's going on with *me*.' He was also writing about Wales and in commenting on its roads said, 'The car has become the most destructive plaything man has ever known.'

On 30 August the *Minerva* berthed at Chatham at the end of her tour of duty and Charles was due for some leave. Prince Philip and Anne had already flown off to Russia and Mark Phillips was with them, nearly a member of the family now. Anne had lost her place in the team after Doublet, who had been nursed back to form, had three refusals at Osberton Trials, near Nottingham, earlier in August. Because of all the political arrangements that had been made, however, Anne went as an individual competitor. She took both Doublet and Goodwill. Anne said on 5 September, at the first day of the championships when she had decided to ride Goodwill, 'He is only a baby at eight years old. The other horses in the top teams are far more experienced. I don't rate my chances.'

On her first day she did well in the dressage, ranking eighth out of twenty-two. But on Saturday 8 September she was thrown and badly bruised. It was a wicked jump and the ground was concrete hard; but when you are competing in top events you must accept those sort of conditions.

Prince Philip and Mark helped her off the course. As she walked away, her face white, she glared at the photographers, busy clicking away, and said to Mark: 'I hope they've got their money's worth now.'

Mark said later: 'The Princess is in good spirits now, although she is unable to move one shoulder. It is stiff and painful.' The Embassy doctor from Moscow was in attendance.

Anne's bitter remarks about the photographers, published in many parts of the world, were inevitably noticed and made the subject of comment. She said on television in the autumn, 'Okay, one says things one doesn't ... one, okay, regrets. But under the heat of the moment, I mean, one was a very disappointed person at that particular moment in time and they were all over the place.'

Charles later came to his sister's defence.

From my sister's point of view, the behaviour of the photographers was very hard to take, and I can understand why. If you are doing something competitive in public, especially in the top international class, you are inevitably keyed up. To have a lot of people with cameras pursuing you, and possibly frightening the horse, is annoying to say the least; and it is easy to become irritable when it is only when things go wrong and you fall off that the gentlemen of the press are interested and that it is only when you are upside down or half-way up a tree that photographs appear in the papers or on TV.

The trouble was, as her father had foreseen, Anne in taking

part publicly in a tough, international sport had come down from the pedestal which protected her and was fair game, and would suffer the more, because of her position.

Prince Andrew was to start at Gordonstoun. The old place had changed quite a lot since Prince Charles was there. As Mr John Kempe commented: 'Just after Prince Charles left a new headmaster – myself – came to the school with new ideas.' New ideas were needed. In spite of the attraction of being the new royal school, many parents who had sent their sons there became disillusioned. Some boys just had to be taken away because they were unhappy. In addition, Gordonstoun did not shine academically at a time when qualifications were becoming more and more important.

Mr Kempe commented: 'Whatever the school's reputation is or was, it is not an extremely Spartan school. We have central heating and a swimming pool heated to seventy-five degrees.' It is now no longer compulsory to take a cold shower in winter.

When Andrew started thirty girl boarders had already been admitted the previous year and it was intended to raise the number to sixty the following year.

Mr Kempe had a valid point in adding that Gordonstoun was no longer exceptional in pushing its pupils out on the hills and to meet the challenge of the seas. This aspect of the Gordonstoun educational system had been widely copied by other schools. He added that Gordonstoun was now no less academically orientated than any other school.

Andrew, who was thirteen, had been given a little more freedom this year. He went to see the League Cup semi-final between Norwich and Chelsea with the Bishop of Norwich, who is often in the pulpit at Sandringham and invited to the house. He went to Cowes for the first time and so did Edward, who was nine. Prince Philip borrowed a racing yacht to give his two younger boys a bit of excitement.

Charles has said that he is not a rebel by temperament. Andrew is another kettle of fish. He was at Balmoral this year when the Queen was presenting new colours to the Scottish regiment on guard duties. As part of the formalities she was asked for permission to march off the old colour, to which she gave the appropriate assent. Andrew was watching with the Queen Mother and said: 'I do wish Mummy would say "No" sometimes!'

Almost as soon as he landed back in England at the end of August Charles became involved in another romance. This time the girl was Lady Jane Wellesley, twenty-two. Lady Jane, only daughter of the Duke of Wellington, was a member of a family which had been one of the most illustrious in Britain since the great Duke had ended the interminable Napoleonic wars on the field of Waterloo.

Since then the dukes who had succeeded him had enjoyed a splendid list of titles only paralleled by those given to John Churchill, first Duke of Marlborough, for destroying the ambitions of another Frenchman, Louis XIV.

Apart from the English Dukedom of Wellington, the head of the Wellesleys is Earl of Mornington in County Meath. The second title is Marquis Douro from the river which flows through Spain and Portugal where the great Duke humbled Napoleon's marshals. He is a Spanish grandee of the first class; marquis and duke in Portugal and prince of Waterloo in the Netherlands. The grateful Spaniards gave a 2,500-acre estate near Granada; the Netherlanders an estate in Belgium. The British nation gave a 10,000-acre estate at Stratfield Saye in Hampshire. By Hyde Park Corner stands the town house, Apsley House, now part residence, part museum in honour of the Duke. There is a Duke of Wellington's Regiment of which the current duke is appointed colonel-in-chief. He is always a governor of Wellington College, created to educate potential officers.

The Dukes of Wellington are pillars of the establishment and have been for generations close to the throne. A Duchess was Mistress of the Robes to Queen Victoria. Lady Jane's grandfather, the seventh Duke who had inherited when his cousin was killed in action at Salerno in 1943, was one of the four Knights of the Garter who had carried the canopy of state at the coronation of Queen Elizabeth in 1953. Lady Jane's father, the present Duke, had commanded the Household Cavalry.

Lady Jane had mixed with the royal family since a child, almost as of right. As part of the circle she had known Charles most of her life. In 1972 he had taken her to the Royal Tournament, but that could have been just a friendly gesture. Now, however, in the autumn of 1973, he was always around or, as would have been said earlier, courting her.

With Anne's wedding taking place on 14 November, Charles's twenty-fifth birthday, there was a certain atmosphere of romance in the air. It was not only Fleet Street which began to speculate. If Charles was to marry a British girl – and there did not seem many suitable candidates among foreign princesses – Lady Jane seemed to fit the bill. Daughter of one of the country's most famous families, good-looking, intelligent, and known all her life to the royal family. It was also pointed out that the Queen Mother had been born a Bowes-Lyon, not nearly so grand a family as the Wellesleys, and had proved one of the most successful consorts in British history.

'Why', it was said, 'dredge up some obscure German princess just to be able to say that Charles was marrying a princess. In any case, hadn't Britain had enough for a long time of the Germans?'

Fleet Street started to publish stories about the friendship pointing out her great eligibility. It was no use her father, the Duke, saying 'utter nonsense' about a possible marriage. Fleet Street still remembered that firm denial about Anne and Mark Phillips.

Jane Wellesley after her education at a boarding school of suitable quality had in 1970 when she was nineteen gone to work for a Fleet Street public relations consultant, Billy Hamilton, whose clients would be impressed by young girls of the aristocracy. Her family bought her a small villa-style house in Hazlebury Road in Fulham where working-class streets were being invaded by the upper classes as prices soared in Chelsea. The house was re-modelled at some expense inside to the Spanish style which Jane had learned to appreciate on her visits to the family estate near Granada. Another girl shared the house for company and Jane settled down to the pattern of life that the girls of her generation and class had adopted.

There were the occasional 'drinks' parties as the old-style cocktail parties were called. Sometimes a dinner-party for a very few friends when a chef would be brought in and, maybe, a waiter and someone to do the washing-up. There was local shopping in the King's Road and Fulham Road, ferreting about for antiques in the Portobello Road. Boyfriends would take her out for a meal in little local restaurants which abounded. There was the local cinema which by now showed the new films, because the film distributors knew where their audience was living. Within a radius of a couple of miles all their friends lived. To that extent it was a 'localized' life, unpretentious even though the delivery vans of Harrods and other shops would appear from time to time.

But, there was another side. As a Wellesley, daughter of the Duke of Wellington, there would be great formal occasions to attend 'all tarted up', as they said. The opera at Covent Garden for special performances; charity concerts with the great musicians performing; diplomatic parties; receptions at the Palace; grand dinner parties at Apsley House. There were week-ends at the great country houses and guests to entertain in the family country-house at Stratfield Saye. There were visits to the Spanish estate, Molino del Rey (Windmill of the King), where a semi-feudal way of life still prevailed with deferential servants and peasant families who bowed as the owners passed by.

It was a curiously mixed life for Jane. On the one hand, the villa in the comparatively humble Fulham street and the job to go to – she was now working in the contemporary art department of Colnaghi's, one of the most prestigious art dealers in London; on the other, still the privileged daughter of a great Duke, meeting on equal terms the royal family and taking part in the grandest social events.

She was at this time described as a stubborn, proud and determined girl – very much the adjectives that were applied to Anne. In Fulham on free evenings she ran up clothes on an old sewing-machine and listened to classical music.

Into this milieu Charles threw himself with enthusiasm and persistence. He had his problems. At a time of terrorist activity – the IRA were extending their activities – he had to be guarded quite closely. There was also a vigilant press. The Fulham neighbours were wonderfully understanding. They could not help noticing, as one of them said later, that he was always in and out of the house that autumn. They seem not, on the whole, to have sold their knowledge to a Fleet Street only too willing to pay.

There was a story printed in the *Sunday Express* that he used to visit Fulham in disguise wearing a beard. The source was a highly inaccurate French scandal sheet, *France Dimanche.* Charles when he was asked about this alleged exploit remarked: 'What a marvellous idea. I wouldn't have believed that the *Sunday Express* could actually believe anything in *France Dimanche.* Those foreign papers will report anything.'

The trouble was that this amused denial did not convince those who recalled that Charles admitted having disguised himself at Cambridge to watch a demonstration. 'I borrowed an overcoat, put up the collar and pulled down a hat over my eyes.' That was not successful: 'I just looked like me trying not to look like me! And everybody kept looking.' Also it was common knowledge that Charles was a great practical joker with an enthusiasm for the Goons and Monty Python. To compensate for the disciplines of his life Charles has developed a side to his life which expresses itself not so much in goonery but fantasy.

Charles had an opportunity in October to talk about the more traditional aspects of British humour. As Earl of Chester he was presenting new colours to the 1st Battalion of the Cheshire Regiment. He told the battalion:

> The extraordinary quality of good humour and tolerance which characterizes the British Army makes it unique and turns the British soldier into an excellent policeman

when circumstances demand. It may not be exactly what you are trained for, or what you joined up for, but you have got this important quality and it is the envy of other countries of the world.

This autumn he also lent his prestige to the Bath Preservation Trust which was trying to save the beauties of the city from the vandals of development and planning. He became its patron and made a gift of £5000.

Meanwhile elaborate plans were being put into operation for the November wedding of Anne and Mark Phillips.

It could not have been a worse time economically, and therefore politically. The Middle East oil-producing countries were feeling their power and, as a start, had quadrupled the price of oil. It affected not only Britain, but all the industrialized countries of Europe, the United States and Japan. It marked the end of the epoch of cheap oil and helped to plunge the world into the worst recession since the thirties. By November a shortage of both oil and coal was developing in Britain. On the thirteenth – the day before the wedding – Mr Heath, the Conservative Prime Minister, declared a state of emergency. The trade figures were alarming. There was panic selling on the Stock Exchange. Industrial relations had deteriorated frighteningly since the Government had set up an Industrial Relations Court which was now sequestrating union assets as a punishment and being accused of being a political court.

It was a time when cool-headed men in positions of power wondered whether national disaster could be averted. Ulster still contributed its daily tale of murder and arson. In London Arab gunmen were using their weapons against prominent Jews. It seemed at times as if the institutions of the country would not be able to take the strain. There were some, on both the extreme right and the extreme left, who were hoping they would not. It was not an easy time for the Queen as she watched and listened. For it was so grave a crisis that the monarchy itself might be involved.

It was not the most appropriate time for wedding-bells.

Since at the wedding the television audience, as with the Prince of Wales's investiture four years earlier, was the primary objective, priority had to be given first to its experts, then to radio and the press. Antony Craxton, who had been at Gordonstoun with Prince Philip, was by now the established BBC producer for royal occasions and was put in charge. The Abbey was taken over many weeks before the event, partially for the erecting of stands for guests, but also to ensure the right facilities for the batteries of TV cameras.

The event deserved its description as 'a marathon TV spectacle'. The BBC programmes ran for eight and a half hours and cost £50,000. Commercial TV gave five hours. The TV pictures were relayed by satellite and by the Eurovision link to the United States, Canada, France, Germany and Australia.

It was estimated that over twenty-seven millions saw the wedding on TV as it happened, and that fifteen millions watched the highlights in the evening. The BBC gave its probable world audience as 550 millions.

The TV coverage started at 8 am with a life of Princess Anne, interviews with people in the streets of London waiting to see the procession, scenes from Mark Phillips's home village of Great Somerford in Wiltshire and a visit to Alison Oliver's stables at Bracknell.

As for radio the BBC world service gave out reports in forty languages.

When to all this is added the reports of British journalists, the corps of journalists who had arrived from all over the world in London, the British and foreign photographers, the resulting coverage was, even by modern standards, awe-inspiring. It made the inauguration of a new President of the United States, for the term of his office the most powerful man in the world, seem a trivial affair.

The Post Office issued two special stamps, based on a photograph taken by the Earl of Lichfield, a professional, who is a cousin of the Queen. The design was used by twenty-four Commonwealth countries.

In Britain there was a national school holiday. In London 4,000 police were on duty; 1,800 members of the services lined the processional route; a party of 21 officers and 213 other ranks were flown over from Mark Phillips's regiment in Germany to line the aisle inside the Abbey and provide a guard of honour outside Buckingham Palace.

It is customary for the services to collect for a gift on the occasion of a royal wedding of such importance. The RAF found its money out of a contingency fund; the navy managed the matter without fuss; but the army, the bridegroom's own service, blundered. In the bad – or good – old days such subscriptions had been made compulsory. In the manner instructions were now issued it seemed as if the tradition was being kept – thirty pence for officers, five pence for other ranks. It reached the ears of the press. There was much unfavourable comment. Mr William Hamilton MP, a well-known scourge of the monarchy, said it was 'a bloody outrage'. He continued, 'If the lads don't fork out, they will be on guard duty and jankers (punishment) and other things.' A second instruction was hurriedly sent out to all units emphasizing that the subscriptions were to be entirely voluntary. The end of the story was that Anne gave a large proportion of the money to charity – in this case mentally handicapped children – and bought herself a Queen Anne chest of drawers with the rest.

Other presents poured in from all over the world. There were over two thousand, including diamonds and rubies. President Tito, the Communist leader of Yugoslavia, to whom the Queen had paid a state visit, sent two of the prized Lippizaner horses. After the wedding the gifts were put on show, together with her wedding-gown, at St James's Palace. There were over 50,000 visitors. The entrance fee was twenty-five pence, the catalogue fifty pence, and the proceeds went to charity.

On the question of money, Anne's income from the Civil List would be automatically increased from £15,000 to £35,000 a year on her marriage. (This had been increased to £50,000 a year by 1977, to compensate for inflation.) Mark Phillips, who was promoted from lieutenant to captain just before the wedding, was to be posted to Sandhurst as an instructor, and a nearby five-bedroomed Georgian house was provided at the ludicrously low rent of £8 a week. This got no better press than the news about the army subscription.

The honeymoon was to be a wonderful cruise in the royal yacht, *Britannia*, which had just had a £2-million refit. Anne and Mark were to fly to Barbados, visit some of the other islands, including Mustique, which Princess Margaret had made well-known, then sail through the Panama Canal and on to the Galapagos Islands, a chain of desert islands and palm-fringed coral islands which is also a famed wildlife paradise. After eighteen days in the yacht, planes from the Queen's Flight would take them on a twelve-day official tour of the West Indies before flying home. There had never been such a splendid honeymoon before. It eclipsed that of Princess Margaret, although she too had had use of the royal yacht.

Mark Phillips remarked just before the wedding: 'Every day people pick up the paper and read about some disaster – I think they are rather relieved to read about something that is genuinely happy and good.'

He was by now indoctrinated into the ways of the royal family. He had spent a week at Balmoral in September where in the magnificent scenery he had been able to observe the Queen, Prince Philip and the family relaxing after the duties of the year and acquire in an informal way something of their attitudes. It was not an easy task for a young man of his background to learn in a few days the easy manners of a royal family. But Anne was there to help him in her brusque, but now very loving fashion.

It had been decided that Mark should wear the full-dress uniform of his regiment. He discovered that no full-dress uniform had been devised for his regiment which was an amalgamation of two others, the Queen's Bays and the King's Dragoon Guards. Full-dress uniform had largely been allowed to lapse in the army since the war because the expense was way beyond the purse of even quite senior officers. However, a uniform was created and many fittings were attended at the tailor's. He would look the part before the television cameras. The uniform will be needed on just a few royal occasions and will then be a notable addition to the new Army Museum in Chelsea.

The wedding-coach had undergone a highly expensive three-month refit. It was the coach used by both the Queen and Princess Margaret for their weddings. Now craftsmen had installed blue silk upholstery. The doors were painted maroon; the chassis glittered, and the crowns at the four corners of the roof were gilded.

Maureen Baker of Susan Small's designed Anne's wedding-dress – which was considered something of a snub for the grand couturiers. It was a sign of the times and Susan Small's had made many dresses for Princess Anne and for Princess Alexandra, two of the most elegant of the royal ladies.

The dress combined all Anne's favourite features. It had a high stand-up neckline, not this time finished with a frill. The torso was tailored and made to fit very rigidly by vertical rows of pin tucks. The sleeves had a narrow head expanding into trailing medieval hangings.

The details were anxiously awaited by the fashion writers and designers who hurriedly made copies for a wider market in Britain and the United States.

Sir John Betjeman wrote some lines for the occasion:

> Hundreds of birds in the air
> And millions of leaves on the pavement.
> Then the bells pealing on
> Over palace and people outside,
> All for the words 'I will'
> To love's most holy enslavement –
> What can we do but rejoice
> With a triumphing bridegroom and bride.

It was Sir John's task as Poet Laureate to produce lines for royal events, but even his admirers were somewhat shaken by this contribution. A Labour MP, Mr Tom Pendry, said the lines were turgid, unromantic and stamped with mediocrity. 'They are the words of an idle scribbler', he said indignantly, 'and he ought to be got rid of.'

Sir John retained one friend in the royal family, however. Two years later Prince Charles, talking about London, said: 'What you need is an expert guide. I always think it would be great fun to go around London with Sir John Betjeman. He's a most amusing man anyway.'

By Monday 12 November, two days before the wedding, the build-up was nearly complete. The guests from abroad were arriving, including a sizeable contingent of German relatives – the Hohenlohe-Langenburgs and the Margrave and Margravine of Baden. Prince Rainier and Princess Grace of Monaco had been invited, although the British royal family had snubbed their own marriage at Monte Carlo.

The Queen was giving a great reception at the Palace that night with 1,500 guests – aristocracy, ministers and politicians, ambassadors, all in evening dress and wearing their decorations with their bejewelled wives in splendid ball-dresses. The orchestras played; the champagne flowed and then the Queen and Prince Philip, with the hundred special guests who had dined with the royal family, came on the scene and opened the ball. It was a scene of fairy-land splendour. Beyond the Palace railings Britain was facing economic and political collapse.

This was also the evening when Anne and Mark appeared on television and gave a forty-three-minute interview to Alastair Burnet of the BBC and Andrew Gardiner of ITV. It had been vetted by the Queen before showing, but there was probably little she could do about it, except scrap it. For Anne was uncompromisingly herself, dominating the scene and scarcely giving Mark Phillips a chance to speak.

She denied that she was either bossy, aloof or 'a swinging princess'. 'People say I'm a bit square, well, fine. I've never pretended to be anything else.' She said she could sew on a button, scramble an egg, took money with her into a shop, did not bet, and did not think much of women's lib.

'No, I don't drink. Nobody believes me. I drink basically coke. Maybe orange or tomato.' Mark Phillips added that neither of them smoked.

He said that he had not been offered a peerage, but was

quite happy as Captain Phillips. Although Anne is close to the throne, therefore, her children, unless the Queen gives Mark a title, will be just plain Phillips.

On the question of where they would like to live Anne said: 'I don't think I am much enamoured with London', calmly dismissing the capital. She added: 'If you are being very impractical about the official life, then I would like to live in Scotland. Well, we may be able to retire to Scotland.'

Mark Phillips scented danger – it might be thought she wanted to retire straightaway – and said, 'Two very old and doddery people.'

They were asked about their hopes for the future. Said Mark Phillips: 'A certain amount of privacy that we may be allowed to have a private life.'

The wedding day came. The clergy were ready in the Abbey, headed by the Archbishop of Canterbury and the Dean of Westminster. The lesson was to be read by the Bishop of Maidstone, the Right Reverend Geoffrey Tiarks, a cousin of the bridegroom.

The guests arrived, among them Richard Meade, the horseman, Olympic Games Gold Medallist, friend of Mark Phillips and, indeed, at one time tipped as a possible match for Anne. There was the blacksmith who shoes Anne's horses and her stable-girl at Alison Oliver's establishment.

The bridegroom looked resplendent in his uniform. His best man had the wedding ring which was made from the residue of a gold nugget found at Dolgellau in Wales which had already provided the wedding rings of the bride's mother, aunt and grandmother.

In came the bride on the arm of her father. Her hair was worn 'à la belle époque'; it shone thick and glossy in a rounded curve at the back under a fine veil. A world-famous make-up artist had flown from Paris to ensure she looked her best. She had only two attendants – her youngest brother, Prince Edward, as page, and Lady Sarah Armstrong-Jones, Princess Margaret's daughter, as bridesmaid.

The ceremony was performed with all the splendour of the Church against a background of music and sweetly-singing choirs. Mark's regimental march, the enlivening *Radetsky March* by Johann Strauss, was played as the couple went down the aisle (it had been appropriately slowed down a little).

Cheering crowds on the way back to the Palace; an appearance on the balcony to wave to the people; a wedding breakfast for a hundred and thirty guests; a drive in an open landau to the Chelsea Hospital; then a car to Thatched House Lodge, Richmond Park (it had been the home of Angus Ogilvy and Princess Alexandra) to spend the first night; the next morning to the airport for the flight to Barbados where the royal yacht waited.

It had been a lavish wedding. When the engagement was announced at the end of May, the elaborate preparations had to be put in train. Anne was the Queen's only daughter. Prince Philip had always had a special devotion to her. In May the economic clouds that darkened the skies in November had not yet gathered in full force.

For the lavishness and great expense at a time of national economic crisis, it would be wrong to blame Anne. Her marriage was a state occasion. It might well be that she would have been just as happy with a simple wedding in a village church with Mark driving her away in a one-horse buggy.

A few days after the wedding Charles had a chance to spend a few days with Lady Jane in Spain. Her parents invited Charles as well as some mutual friends – Lord Plunket, deputy master of the Queen's Household, and Lord Porchester, the Queen's racehorse manager. There was good food and wine and excellent shooting. It also gave Charles and Lady Jane time together far away from the crowds.

The press, British and foreign, drew the conclusion that the relationship was deepening and should be taken seriously. Charles spent Christmas with his family at Sandringham. They invite a few guests for the New Year celebrations and this time one of them was Lady Jane. This seemed to clinch the matter for the press and there was a wave of stories predicting an imminent engagement. There was a crowd of nearly ten thousand sightseers waiting to see the royal family attend the local church on the Sunday. Charles escorted Lady Jane.

On 2 January 1974, both Charles and Jane left Sandringham. She was going back to work in London. He was flying to Singapore to join his new ship, the frigate *Jupiter*, for a three months' tour of the Pacific.

The expected announcement was not made then or later.

In March 1974, the *Sun* wrote of her, 'The girl tipped to be the next Queen of England', and many other newspapers were of the same opinion. A few days later she appeared with the Queen Mother and Princess Alexandra as the third lady in the royal party at a Royal Film Première. It was as if some of the royal family were still hoping. If so, it was in vain.

9

Shootings in the Mall

Prince Charles was appointed Communications Officer in the *Jupiter* and to keep in touch set up a radio exercise with his regiment, the Royal Regiment of Wales, back in Europe which he, at any rate, thought 'gave some useful inter-service experience and training'. At sea he found time for reading and devoured a lot of history and biographies. 'I'm also fascinated', he said, 'by some of the books by Alexander Solzhenitsyn. The *Gulag Archipelago*, his latest one, is riveting in many ways and horrifying, utterly horrifying. And most moving.'

He indulged his taste for practical jokes. A shipmate said afterwards that he never stopped playing pranks. Once he hid in a large cardboard container in the wardroom and then suddenly emerged and showered his fellow-officers with syphons of soda water and custard pies.

The *Jupiter* made calls in Australia, New Zealand and the South Seas Islands before making for the West Coast of the United States and Mexico. The Royal Navy is generally welcome when it calls, but with the Prince of Wales aboard officers and men found the hospitality overflowing. 'We had a wonderful time', said one of the crew. 'We were treated like royalty ourselves. We never had to pay for anything.'

This certainly helped his popularity on board, although he was well-liked for himself and the lower-deck gave him a nickname, always a good sign. It was 'Taffy Windsor'.

On visits ashore Prince Charles was naturally the guest of honour at the receptions and dinners. He was now self-assured and a good mixer, giving his views on most subjects. For example, on Frank Sinatra, 'He can be terribly nice at one moment and not so nice the next – and I am not impressed by the creeps and Mafia types he keeps around with.'

In March the *Jupiter* was to pay a courtesy call for a few days at San Diego, an important American port and naval station on the West Coast. Here the Americans laid on royal hospitality for all. There were parties, receptions, tours and everything a sailor dreams of at sea. Nothing was too good for Charles and he was introduced to an admiral's daughter, Laura Jo Watkins, a beautiful girl of twenty, who showed him the sights. For her they were unforgettable days.

When the *Jupiter* sailed away, weary, but shipshape, many had pleasant memories of San Diego. Charles was to find in a few months that his memory would be refreshed in London.

The frigate sailed south towards the Panama Canal, but put in first at Acapulco in Mexico, renowned for its wine, women and song.

Charles was suddenly called away urgently from the festivities to take a call from London. His sister Anne had that evening, a few hundred yards from Buckingham Palace, barely escaped with her life from a man armed with two revolvers who intended to kidnap her and hold her to ransom.

It was 20 March 1974.

Anne and Mark Phillips had been guests of honour at a special showing of a film, *Riding Towards Freedom*, about riding for the disabled in which Anne takes an interest. The Duke of Norfolk welcomed them. At the end of the showing in Sudbury House, Newgate Street, near Ludgate Circus, Anne and Mark drove away to return to the Palace. It was about 7.40 pm. The car crossed Trafalgar Square and moved swiftly along the Mall, by now emptying of traffic, and made towards the Palace. Just beyond St James's Palace, which is on the right, a light-coloured Ford Escort turned sharply in front of the royal car, an Austin Princess, and forced it to stop.

There were five people in the royal car. In front were Mr Alexander Callender, the chauffeur, and Inspector James Beaton, the Princess's bodyguard. In the back were Anne and

Mark with the lady-in-waiting, Rowena Brassey, who was on a folding seat.

James Beaton got out to see what had happened. He went round the back of the car and as he appeared on the off-side a young, neatly-dressed man wearing gloves, who was trying to open the rear door nearest to Princess Anne, raised a gun and shot him in the chest. Beaton drew his gun – all royal bodyguards are armed – fired, missed, tried to fire again, but his weapon jammed. Rowena Brassey opened the further rear door, got out and crouched on the ground. By now the man had opened the door nearest to Anne, caught hold of her, and said: 'Please get out of the car.' Mark Phillips held on to her. The man then told Beaton to put down his gun otherwise he would shoot Anne. Beaton, with a useless gun, complied. Mark Phillips had managed to shut the door while this exchange went on. The man shouted: 'Open the door or I'll shoot!' He now had a second gun. Beaton put his hand directly in front of the muzzle as the man fired into the car. The bullet hit his hand. Beaton, now wounded twice, opened the door and pushed it against the man, hoping to knock him over. The man shot him a third time, this time in the stomach. Beaton collapsed on the road. The chauffeur, Alexander Callender, now made to get out of the driving seat. The man told him to stay where he was and switch off the engine. Callender got out, grabbed the man's right arm, and was shot in the chest.

A police constable, Michael Hills, on duty by St James's Palace, had heard the shots, ran over and tried to get the man's gun from him. In the struggle he was shot in the stomach. Before collapsing he managed to say over his pocket radio, 'There's shooting. I've been shot.'

Brian McConnell, a Fleet Street journalist, was in a taxi held up behind the royal car. He got out, walked up to the man and said: 'Look, old man, these are friends of mine. Don't be silly: just give me the gun.' The man raised it and shot McConnell in the chest.

Mr Ronald Russell, who had been driving by, got out of his car, punched the man, who fired at him and missed.

By now police cars, alerted by the radio call, were flooding

Thai classical dancers lay petals at the feet of Anne during a visit to the Far East with her parents in February 1972.

Anne became engaged to Mark Phillips on 29 May 1973. The Queen and Prince Philip, Major and Mrs Phillips pose for a family photograph.

Here comes the bride — on the arm of her father.

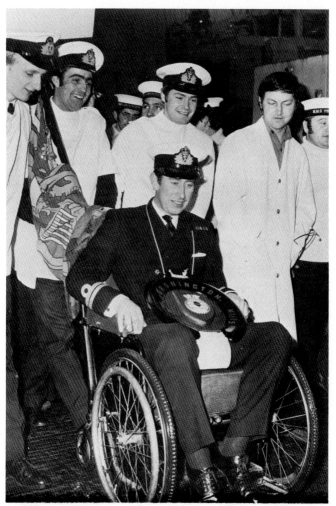

Charles left the navy in December 1976 after five years' service. He was wheeled ashore by the officers and ratings of HMS *Bronington* which he had commanded, adorned with a lavatory seat and toilet paper.

Andrew in Canada where he had gone to spend six months at
Lakefield College in 1977.

During a visit to Ghana in 1977 Charles was invested in ritual robes as
Naba Nampasa — one who helps mankind.

Andrew and Edward with their grandmother, the Queen Mother, at the
service in St Paul's on 7 June 1977 which marked the national
thanksgiving for the Queen's Silver Jubilee.

Andrew went back to Canada in July 1977 for a ten-day adventure holiday.

Princess Anne's baby has just been christened Peter at Buckingham Palace. The Queen raises a laugh from her first grandchild.

THE GIRLS IN CHARLES'S LIFE

Lucia Santa Cruz: the Cambridge companion.

The talented Georgiana Russell.

Lady Jane Wellesley: 'I hope he liked me, but I really can't say.'

The captivating Davina Sheffield.

Lady Sarah Spencer , kinswoman of the Churchills.

The Czech Countess Angelika Lazansky, a guest at Balmoral.

£16 million raised for the Queen's Silver Jubilee Fund — Charles announces the record result.

An exotic interlude in Rio de Janeiro — Charles learns the samba.

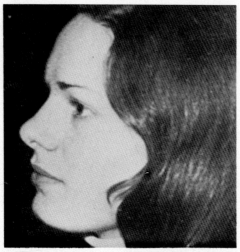

A girlfriend for Andrew, now 18, at Sandringham. Kirsty Richmond, a fellow-pupil at Gordonstoun.

A family conference: Charles, Andrew and Edward discussing form at the North Warwickshire hunt. With Andrew is Clio Nathaniels, another friend from Gordonstoun.

into the Mall. An unarmed detective constable, Peter Edmunds, brought the man down with a rugby tackle and seized him.

On the other side of the car where Rowena Brassey was crouching she was joined by Miss Samantha Scott, a young dancing instructress, who had been driving behind in her mini. She went up to Miss Brassey who said, 'Keep your head down. There's a maniac firing.'

We huddled on the ground. I could see Mark Phillips protecting Anne while the man tried to get them. They were huddled on the ground. I could see yellow roses scattered over the floor of the car.

When the gunman had gone, I opened the door of the car and put my hand on Anne's shoulder. I said to her, 'Are you all right, love?' She replied sweetly, 'I'm all right, thank you.' I asked Mark Phillips if he was OK and he said, 'I'm fine, thank you.'

Back in the Palace, Anne put through a call to the Queen and Prince Philip who were in Indonesia. Another call was put through to Prince Charles in Mexico.

Anne issued a brief statement from the Palace:

We are very thankful to be in one piece. But we are deeply disturbed and concerned about those who got injured, including our chauffeur and Inspector Beaton. Inspector Beaton acted particularly bravely and although already shot he continued to protect us. We are extremely grateful to all those members of the police and public who tried to help us.

In the House of Commons the Home Secretary, Mr Roy Jenkins, interrupted proceedings to make a statement.

Sir Robert Mark, the Commissioner of the Metropolitan Police, visited the wounded in hospital later in the evening. It could have been worse. All survived, even Inspector Beaton.

The same evening Mr Edward Short (later Lord Glenamara), then Leader of the House, said he had seen 'a kidnap letter' addressed to the Queen. It was 'a very long letter demanding ransom'.

The name of the man being questioned, and then charged, was given as Mr Ian Ball, aged twenty-six, an Englishman living in North London.

The news disturbed the nation. The press next day reflected alarm, and relief that Anne was safe. The normally sober *Times* had an almost hysterical leader, 'A Symbol of Hatred'. It began:

> The attack on Princess Anne and Captain Mark Phillips is not only a brutal physical attack on a young married couple, but also is itself an attack on the idea of Britain, a gesture of hatred as well as an act of hatred.
>
> It is a symbol of the world into which we have moved, a world increasingly ruthless and increasingly irrational, a world in which the principle of order is by its nature exposed to furious attack, and any individual, however innocent, who seems to symbolize order or grace is liable to attack for that reason.
>
> There are people about who hate civilization because it exists ... They hate us very much, but most of all they hate anything good about us.

British phlegm was disturbed this year of 1974. In an atmosphere of industrial and economic disaster, Mr Heath, the Conservative Prime Minister, had called an election in February – and just lost. Mr Wilson formed a Labour government and got Britain back to work from a three-day week, but at the expense of large and highly inflationary wage settlements. The IRA terrorists of Ulster had spread their activities to England. Appeals for a regime of 'law and order' found a response in many hearts. The vaunted British democracy looked shaky.

The public was naturally dismayed at the ease with which one man had been able so easily to evade security and come within an ace of killing or kidnapping the Queen's daughter. The police and security men had always known that it could happen. They did their best, in the framework of an open society, to give protection. But there was a mood abroad that was leading to a wave of kidnappings and murders, and each act fostered others through the publicity it was given. Scotland Yard knew there was always a possibility of failure of their security measures, especially if the attacker was a loner and deranged.

This is what Ian Ball proved to be when he was brought for trial before the Lord Chief Justice on 22 May.

Already at a preliminary appearance at Bow Street on 28 March Ball's solicitor had stated: 'It should be known in the interest of the defendant and the public generally that the defendant has a confirmed history of psychiatric illness. He was diagnosed in hospital in 1967 as a schizoid and he is being examined at the moment by eminent psychiatrists.' On 4 April at another appearance a statement by Ball said: 'I did it because I wished to draw the public attention to the lack of facilities for treating mental illness under the National Health Service.'

When the trial opened Ball pleaded guilty to trying to kidnap Princess Anne in the Mall, attempting to murder two policemen, and wounding two civilians.

The Attorney-General, Mr Samuel Silkin, appeared for the prosecution. He said: 'There can be no doubt that the defendant Ball conceived over many years a horrifying plan which he prepared with almost obsessive care and detail to kidnap single-handed in the heart of London a member of the royal family.'

The attempt, he continued, had nothing to do with any revolutionary or extremist group.

Ian Ball had been born in 1948 in Watford, north of London, son of a fitter. He grew up a solitary young man and at the age of twenty left home. He took various jobs, mainly as a van driver. He lived austerely which left him with money to indulge in pursuits which might have seemed beyond his means. He took flying lessons at Biggin Hill and obtained a pilot's licence. In 1968 he had two convictions for trying to auction a stolen car and then selling parts from another stolen car. In 1970 he went to live in a bed-sitter at Hazel Court in Bayswater. He was quiet, regular in his habits, and repulsed any attempts at friendship, even acquaintanceship. In December 1973 he went to Spain and bought two revolvers for £80 and some ammunition. He brought them back unchallenged through the Customs at Heathrow Airport.

In February 1974 he asked a member of a firm of solicitors, Dale and Newbery, of Hounslow, to draw up an agreement about an unexplained criminal matter. His purpose was to use them as an intermediary in the ransom demand.

In March, under the name of Mr Van der Fluis, he rented a house, 17 Silverdale Road at Fleet in Hampshire, not far from Sandhurst where Princess Anne was living with her husband. It was a middle-class house in a quiet cul-de-sac. He obtained it from estate agents at Frimley, giving good references, paying £100 in cash for four weeks' rent and also a deposit for the six months' contract. A few of the residents tried to make a social approach. He rebuffed them. The neighbours remarked that he played classical music on a record-player very loud and very late.

When the police raided the house after the kidnap attempt the kitchen was well-stocked with tins of ham, pork, luncheon meat and coffee. It would have provided for several people for some days.

Ball then hired a Ford Escort car in Stepney, London, using a driving licence in the name of John Williams. In Camberley, Surrey, near Fleet, he hired a typewriter, attracting attention because he wanted it for one day only.

On this machine the ransom letter to the Queen was typed 'immaculately on foolscap'. It was described as 'very long and rambling'. At the trial part of the letter was read out. It began:

> Your daughter has been kidnapped. The following are the conditions for her release. A ransom of £3m is to be paid in £5 notes. They are to be used, unmarked, not sprayed with any chemical substance, and inconsecutively numbered.
>
> The money is to be packed in thirty unlocked suitcases clearly marked on the outside. The following documents are to be prepared: a free pardon to cover the kidnapping and

anything connected with it, i.e., the possession of firearms or the murder of any police officers. A free pardon for any crimes committed by myself, from parking offences to murder. As the money is to be banked abroad, I shall be asking for a free pardon to run indefinitely for being in contravention of the Exchange Control Act.

Documents are to be prepared for a civilian action to be taken against the police if they disclose my true identity for damages of not less than £1m. A civilian action to be taken against you or your consorts if you reveal my true identity. No excuses will be accepted for failing to compile these documents. If they cannot be drawn up under existing laws, the laws must be changed.

On the week-end before the kidnapping Ball drove his car to a road near Oak Grove House, where Anne and Mark Phillips were living. A servant noted it on four separate days parked 250 yards from the rear gate. It was also seen on Wednesday the twentieth, the day of the kidnapping.

On that same day, around lunchtime, a senior police officer – a detective chief inspector – stopped and questioned Ball, thinking he might have been connected with a local burglary. Ball gave the name of Williams and a driving licence in that name. The car was searched and nothing found.

Seven hours later Ian Ball swerved his car in front of Princess Anne's limousine in the Mall and made his kidnap attempt. He had with him two guns, ammunition, four pairs of handcuffs, their keys and the ransom letter. He also had on him £569 in cash.

Ball's defence counsel at the trial, Mr John Hazan QC, said the attempt had been made by a single, sick man. Ian Ball had felt that an act of God had told him to swerve in front of the car. Counsel asked for an order committing his client to hospital on four grounds: that Mr Ball was mad at the time; he was still potentially suicidal and homicidal; he needed treatment; and there was a secure hospital available.

The Lord Chief Justice, Lord Widgery, ordered Ball to be

detained in a hospital under the Mental Health Act 'without limit of time'. He added: 'I accept the evidence of the doctors that he requires treatment.'

He also said: 'My concern which may perhaps be exercised in the future rather than today, is that when this kind of offence is becoming more serious and more common in the world the time may come when we have to recognize that for offences such as this the background of a prison sentence is necessary to secure maximum protection for the public.'

The Attorney-General in his opening remarks had said this was a case where truth was stranger than fiction. It was and yet it was reassuring to the public that such an act would only be committed by a madman. A cynic might say it was almost too convenient to be true. Presumably the quite considerable sum of money expended by Ball and in his possession had come from, say, car thefts of which he had been shown to have experience. His meticulous timing of the hold-up in the Mall could, presumably, have been carried out by reading information in the press of the Princess's engagement that evening and timing her return. Certainly, it seemed strange that the letter was so immaculately typed – not an easy task in a long letter for someone who had no record of skilled typing.

However, there the matter rests.

The Queen, with general approbation, recognized the bravery of the men involved. James Beaton received the George Cross, the civilian equivalent of the VC. Michael Hills and Ronald Russell were given the George Medal, which ranks second to the Cross. Brian McConnell, Alexander Callender and Peter Edmunds were awarded the Queen's Gallantry Medal.

On Anne's birthday, 15 August, the Queen created her daughter Dame Grand Cross of the Royal Victorian Order (the sovereign's personal order) and expressed her admiration for the Princess's calm and brave behaviour throughout the incident. Mark Phillips was made a Commander of the same Order and Rowena Brassey, a member of the Fourth Class.

On 26 November the Queen gave a special investiture for

the men who had helped to save her daughter's life. There was a party afterwards to which their families had been invited. Princess Anne and Mark Phillips were there to give their thanks.

While Charles was still overseas with HMS *Jupiter* it was announced from London that he had accepted the presidency of the British Sub-Aqua Club. He had practical reasons for encouraging the Club. In the Royal Navy he had gone through a diving course and practised the submarine escape procedures.

Jupiter berthed at Plymouth on 22 April after a 96,000-mile tour. Charles did not let the opportunity pass for another practical joke. On the quayside was a minibus marked 'For officers of HMS *Jupiter*'. The destination board read: 'HM Tower of London'.

Soon after Charles also suffered a physical attack when he went on an underwater warfare course at Portland. One night a naval lieutenant crashed into his sitting-room and started to heave furniture about. Charles woke up and went into the room. The officer was about to hit him with a chair when he was seized by the Prince's bodyguard. An inquiry was held and it was found that the officer was suffering from mental trouble.

In the same month, April, the Prime Minister announced that the Prince of Wales had decided to take up the option of taking possession of the large and beautiful country mansion of Chevening, near Chipstead in Kent. Lord Stanhope, a man of great wealth, had left the house, built by Inigo Jones in the seventeenth century, and the estate of 3,500 acres, which in-included four farms and 400 acres of woodlands, to the descendants of George VI in the hope that it might become the country home of the Prince of Wales. The trustees also had available £250,000 for rehabilitation which was needed as the house had been scarcely touched inside since 1900.

At first, the royal family, including Prince Charles, did not seem anxious to take up this generous gift. Lord Stanhope had arranged that if the royal family did not want it, the house and estate should be made available to Cabinet Ministers, or, finally, to the National Trust. In fact, Lord Hailsham, Lord Chancellor in Mr Heath's government, did occupy a flat at Chevening for a time.

Prince Charles finally decided to accept this princely house and estate, which Lord Rosebery, the Liberal Prime Minister, who owned Mentmore no less, had described as 'a paradise'.

A complete rehabilitation programme had been in progress since 1970 and before Charles finally took possession around £1 million had been spent on the eighty rooms. Lady Thorneycroft, Italian-born and an expert in interior decoration, had been employed for a time on the task. Dr Roy Strong, the Director of the Victoria and Albert Museum, was called in to advise. Prince Charles has had the entire house wired for sound as he likes to be able to switch on music in every room, including the lavatories.

There was criticism of Charles's taking the house, as he soon realized. It was felt that Charles was rich enough with his Duchy of Cornwall's revenues to buy his own place and that the royal family already owned more than enough houses and estates. Kenneth Harris asked Charles if he thought his image had been improved by the reports that he was going to live at Chevening – obviously a leading question, under the circumstances.

Charles replied:

Apparently not. But when I accepted the offer it was a home of my own that was offered to me, not an improvement in my image ... If I'd bought a poky little house of my own, I think I would also have come in for criticism; if I'd bought a big house out of my own pocket I would have come in for more criticism. Some people have said that the house should be opened to the public or put to some other use. As the house has not been touched since 1900 there is a lot to do to it inside – even if it were opened to the public – so it would seem better for the house to be lived in by someone who would enjoy it and use it as it should be used than to end up as a lifeless museum, which was not what Lord Stanhope wanted.

Charles had a notable duty soon after his return to England. He was asked to speak at a presentation to the Fellows of the Churchill Trust. He said that he had met Churchill when he was a boy at Balmoral. Churchill was sitting by Loch Muick on the estate. When Charles approached him, he looked up and said: 'I'm waiting for the Loch Ness Monster.' Of the great man Charles had some well-chosen words: 'He was able to use words in the way Mozart used musical notes.'

On his return to England Charles had not renewed his close friendship with Lady Jane Wellesley. Another girl had captivated him. She was Davina Sheffield, then twenty-three, whom he had met at a dinner party given by Lady Jane. History was repeating itself. The Duke of Windsor had met the then Mrs Wallis Simpson at a dinner party given by his reigning girlfriend, Thelma, Viscountess Furness.

Davina was the daughter of Major George Sheffield, third son of Sir Berkeley Sheffield Bt. The family baronetcy had been created in the first part of the eighteenth century to provide for the illegitimate son of the Duke of Buckingham and Normanby. The legitimate line became extinct in 1732 and the Duke left the estates to his mistress's son. Davina's mother, Agnes, was the younger daughter of Lord McGowan, who was one of the great industrial tycoons of the inter-war years who had built up ICI into a giant organization. Both Davina's parents had been married before. Davina had a sister, Laura, two years older, who was married to George Pilkington, a stockbroker. She had known Princess Anne for some time.

Davina had been a débutante and given all the advantages of girls belonging to her world. The family is related to Mrs Keppel, the mistress of King Edward VII.

Davina and Laura led the contemporary life of their kind. They had a house in Gertrude Street which lies between the King's Road and the Fulham Road. They had a rather amateurish shop on Chelsea Green called Munster Arcade which sold Irish cottage industry products, basketwork and flower pots.

Davina was attractive, much sought after, went to parties,

dinners in the Chelsea–Fulham area and weekends away. Charles began to spend a lot of time with her.

In June Charles's personal relationships became somewhat complicated. Mr Walter Annenberg, the very rich American ambassador, and his wife, invited Laura Jo ('L.J.') Watkins, the American admiral's daughter, to stay with them, having heard about her whirlwind friendship with Prince Charles at San Diego earlier in the year.

Charles was in duty bound to extend hospitality. Her arrival caused some consternation. The *Daily Telegraph*, a serious-minded newspaper, had an article on the friendship and pointed out the constitutional difficulties that would arise if he wanted to marry her since she was a Roman Catholic.

'L.J.' was given a seat to watch the Queen at the Trooping the Colour ceremony on Horse Guards Parade. She was given a place in the House of Lords galleries to hear Charles make his maiden speech with great confidence after expressing modestly 'some degree of fear and trepidation'. She saw Charles at Kensington Palace. Then the visit seemed to fizzle out.

Back in America she bravely said, 'I had a fantastic time.' But it was said that she also felt that the press publicity had stopped her being received by the Queen and caused the cancellation of a weekend at Balmoral.

The visit was an embarrassment, especially for the American girl who seemed a particularly nice person. Probably the Annenbergs had been misguided in furthering the visit. 'L.J.' was not snubbed, but nearly.

However, Charles had another girl he wished his mother to entertain at Balmoral – Davina Sheffield. She was invited. She was seen with Charles when the royal family went to Crathie Church on Sunday.

Charles had been spending much time with her, not only in London. She had gone with him to a small village on the coast he had got to know when he was at Dartmouth. They were seen surfing and relaxing.

In August Charles finally left *Jupiter* at Rosyth. He had now completed altogether eighteen months' sea service and was looking forward to a three months' course the following month at Yeovil to train as a helicopter pilot.

Davina and her sister, Laura, sold the shop on Chelsea Green in August. It had not been doing well and the man who took it over was embarrassed by the amount of unsold stock including several hundred teddy bears which he passed on to a children's charity. Davina went on holiday in the South of France. James Beard was with her. He is an ex-Harrovian who designs power-boats and had long been close to Davina. At one time they were 'unofficially engaged'. He has been quite forthcoming about Davina, describing how she often visited him at his cottage in England, and he has praised her many qualities, including cooking.

Charles had had enough emotional experiences one way and another this year to make him thoughtful.

In June he was talking about marriage to Kenneth Harris who was suggesting that it would be unlikely for him to marry somebody who was not of a royal family or a member of the aristocracy.

'There's no essential reason why I shouldn't', replied Charles. 'I'd be perfectly free to. What would make it unlikely would be accidental, not essential.' Going on to talk about the lasting nature of marriage he added, 'So I'd want to marry somebody who had interests which I understood and could share.' He then looked at it from the woman's point of view:

> A woman not only marries a man; she marries into a way of life, into a job, into a life in which she's got a contribution to make. She's got to have some knowledge of it, some sense of it, or she wouldn't have a clue about whether she's going to like it, and if she didn't have a clue, it would be risky for her, wouldn't it?

By the end of the year when he was talking to Stuart Kuttner, he sounded a more worldly-wise note:

> But I do feel this: a lot of people get the wrong idea about what love is all about. I think it is more than just a rather romantic, glamorous idea about falling madly in

love with somebody and having a love affair for the rest of your married life. In many cases one falls madly in 'love' with somebody with whom you are in fact infatuated rather than in love.

My marriage has to be forever.

When he was asked if he had any particular girl to marry in mind at that time, he replied, 'Obviously there are certain people I've thought of on those lines. But, no, I wouldn't say anybody in particular at this moment.'

There is room for sympathy with Charles in the problems of his emotional life. Compared with, say, the inter-war years, details of the life of the royal family are much more openly published and commented on. Charles's romances are not censored by the press as were those of his predecessor as Prince of Wales, the Duke of Windsor. It is a more open society and by and large the monarchy has benefited from the enlargement of public knowledge about the royal family. The nation has been able to identify with it. If this process had been thwarted, there would have been a danger that the royal family would gradually have been considered not much more than a remote group of privileged men and women who were brought out now and again in ceremonial clothes to perform hierarchical duties and utter pious platitudes according to a prescribed ritual. The monarchy would have become superfluous.

On the other hand, it has meant that whole areas of personal life that would once have been protected by the writ of 'private' have become public. In becoming more public the private life of the royal family has become more circumscribed. It has brought strains on some members of the royal family which they consider intolerable. Princess Anne is a case in point.

While Charles was on his helicopter course, he was able to do a good turn for one of his favourite goons. Harry Secombe had written a novel, *Twice Brightly*, and Charles wrote an enthusiastic review for *Punch* calling it 'a compendium of Welsh wit and thespianism'.

About this time he also referred to the influx of girls at Gordonstoun and said his brother, Andrew, who was fourteen, was 'enjoying himself immensely' – which was more than could be said of his own Gordonstoun days.

They were saying of Andrew that he was 'almost the split image of his father at his age'. He was growing tall (he would be nearly six feet); blonde, blue-eyed, with an aggressive charm. He was a good all-round sportsman and Prince Philip said he was 'a natural boss'.

His mother, the Queen, however, remarked that he was not always a little ray of sunshine. Among his practical jokes had been climbing on to the roof of Buckingham Palace and 'adjusting the TV aerial and pouring bath essence into the swimming-pool at Windsor. In a dormitory fight at school he had got a crack on the head which put him into hospital for a couple of days.

One of his masters said: 'He's a very tough and independent fellow. He has no time for sycophants. He's good – just as good – with verbalistics as he is with his fists.'

Anne and Mark Phillips had a busy year in the leading riding events. At Badminton Anne swept into the lead for dressage on faithful Doublet. In May, however, Doublet, now eleven years old, who had given Anne her great successes, broke a leg while she was riding him at Windsor and had to be destroyed. It affected her deeply.

Just before the Burghley events Anne gave an interview to the BBC and was asked what was the right age to give up competitive riding. 'When you lose your nerve', she replied. 'It shouldn't take long.' She added: 'You need a lot of luck, quite a large dollop of it as far as I'm concerned', and she admitted having 'moments of terror on a horse'.

The family gathered at Sandringham for Christmas, conscious that they were lucky to have Anne with them after the kidnap attempt. The big house at Sandringham was being modernized at a cost of £200,000 and a large farmhouse, Wood Farm, had been made ready. Early in the New Year the Queen suspended the new works for the time being. She was having to ask Parliament for another large increase to compensate for the galloping inflation. Everyone was feeling the pinch.

Enterprise in Canada

Charles finished his helicopter course at Yeovilton, completing 105 flying hours in 45 days. When he was asked what he had enjoyed most in his naval career, he replied. 'I can safely say the helicopter course. I adore flying and I personally can't think of a better combination than naval flying – being at sea and being able to fly. I find it very exciting, very rewarding and stimulating. Also bloody terrifying sometimes!'

He spoke of the risks: 'Many people forget that a helicopter is an inherently unstable machine. With a helicopter you've got to expect something to go wrong any minute and be ready to do something about it pretty quickly because if you don't you drop like a stone.'

Charles did not mention that he had been in two forced helicopter landings. Nothing had damped his enthusiasm. 'Commando flying, rocket flying and landing on carriers and the back end of ships in howling gales.' He commented: 'I found the course easier and I got the knack more quickly than I had thought.'

He had evenings out with his fellow pilots. One was at Oke-hampton and the press reported that they had searched for a strong cider, 'scrumpy'.

'I think', said Charles, 'that as the whole thing was in the Duchy of Cornwall area that added to the chances of pub-licity. Everybody instantly recognized me in the pubs. Mar-vellous old boys in caps came up and said: "Like ter shake yer 'and." They were charming. One old boy produced his Home Guard certificate signed by my grandfather. But that sort of thing never gets reported', added Charles a little bitterly. 'It's all this business about looking for scrumpy. Everyone must think I'm an alcoholic.'

After the helicopter training, Charles was sent to the Royal Marine Commando Training Centre at Lympstone in Devon to do an assault course. 'Part of our duties as helicopter pilots', he explained, 'involves carrying Royal Marines. And it's considered a good idea for the pilots to find out what the Marines have to put up with.' He also went through a 'Tarzan' course. He described it in vivid terms to Stuart Kuttner:

A most horrifying expedition where you have to swing over small chasms on ropes, slide down ropes at death-defying speeds and then walk across wires and up rope ladders strung between a pole and a tree. And all those sort of ghastly things. Anyway, I survived that and came out with my knees trembling in fear and trepidation. Then we had to do a form of survival course this afternoon which involved crawling through tunnels half filled with water, then running across the moor and back.

The zest and humour with which Charles described what is, by any standards, a tough course, was becoming typical of his attitude to life. He said later this year of 1975, 'I like trying my hand at things and if people say do you want to have a go, I usually say yes.'

For those who had known the Charles of the early years at Cheam and Gordonstoun the change seemed little more than a revolution. The change had stemmed from Timbertop in Australia.

Charles was posted as a helicopter pilot to 845 Naval Air Squadron which was to do a tour of duty in the commando ship, *Hermes*, in the Atlantic and West Indies.

Before he joined her he went to Nepal with Lord Mountbatten for the coronation of King Birendra. The ceremonies in Katmandu, the capital of the mountain kingdom bounded by Tibet and India, had a dream-like quality of oriental magic and beauty. Nepal provides the famous Gurkha regiments which have fought valiantly in Britain's wars. The links are still there and for Lord Mountbatten, who had been Supreme

Commander in South-East Asia in the final campaign against Japan, it was a time for happy reminiscence. Time was found for a brief visit to India, where Lord Mountbatten had been the last viceroy and master-minded the transference of power to two new states, India and Pakistan. The visits to India and Nepal were part pleasure for Charles, and part an extension of experience.

Back in London Charles addressed the House of Commons press gallery before going to sea. He decided to talk to them about the marriage rumours linking him with Lady Jane. Referring to his friendship with 'a certain young lady', he said: 'Such was the obvious conviction that what they had read was true that I almost felt that I had better espouse myself at once, so as not to disappoint too many people. As you can see, I thought better of it.'

There was a certain insensitivity in his remarks. It was as if the toughening up of Charles had led to the loss of his former care for the feelings of others. He had said previously, 'Jane is a jolly nice girl and I really pity her about the publicity.' Yet here he was bringing it all up again before an audience of journalists.

'Poor Jane Wellesley', as he had referred to her, behaved with dignity in a disagreeable situation. At the end of this year, 1975, she said, for publication in the *Daily Express*: 'I don't know whether I'm to be included among the girls Prince Charles is supposed to have fallen in love with. You had better ask him. I hoped he liked me, but I really can't say.'

While Charles was talking about Lady Jane, Davina Sheffield had broken loose from her Chelsea moorings. The Vietnam war was reaching its final stages as the Americans withdrew leaving a corrupt government, disaffected troops and an appalling refugee situation which was brought vividly home to the world by television.

Davina Sheffield decided she ought to do something about it. She flew to Saigon, a despairing city filled with the human debris of the long and, even by the standards of this century, cruel war. There were thousands of children, many injured, all in want. Davina applied to various relief organizations which were battling with the problem. But she was turned down for lack of professional experience. However, a Danish journalist, who had received funds to help, opened an orphanage for around sixty children and Davina was welcome there. Among the journalists she got a name as a girl of courage who cheerfully took on any task, however menial or distressing.

By April the Communists were nearing the city and the evacuation of foreigners was hastened. Davina said: 'I feel a real sense of purpose here and I don't want to leave.' But she saw reason and finally left. She went first to Thailand and then made her way to Australia before returning later in the year to England.

Some of her friends thought she had shown guts and a sincere wish to do good. Others dismissed the episode as a romantic fantasy in which she had seen herself playing a heroic role. Whatever they thought she returned somewhat chastened by her experiences.

Charles went to the frozen north this spring. Service training in Arctic conditions has become important since war over the northern polar regions became a possibility. He underwent a ten-day course in the Arctic islands on Resolute Bay in northern Canada. During the survival programme he had to swim for half an hour under the ice in an inflatable suit. He described the experience light-heartedly: 'I sank like a great orange walrus into the ice-covered world below.' He finally floated up, 'looking exactly like M. Michelin.'

It was seen from the photographs that he had grown a beard – a sensible protection and one which made him resemble many of his ancestors here and abroad.

Anne and Mark Phillips were at Badminton as usual in the spring. Anne came fifteenth in the dressage on the first day, but Mark Phillips's mount, Persian Holiday, was injured. However, the event turned out a disaster; torrential rain fell and it had to be abandoned.

Charles was given more dignities this year. He was appointed Colonel-in-Chief of the Welsh Guards on 1 March, St David's Day, and was installed by the Queen as Grand Master of the Most Honourable Order of the Bath on 25 May. The ceremony was held in the magnificent Henry VII Chapel (chapel of the Order) in Westminster Abbey. Charles wore the magnificent robes with *élan* and it was noticed that though the beard had gone, a moustache remained.

He had an opportunity of paying tribute to the Mountbattens and the Fleet Air Arm in a preface to a new history of the service. 'Pride swells in my heart yet again when I recall the part played by my great-grandfather, Prince Louis, in the formation of the Royal Naval Air Service in 1914.' (Prince Louis was First Sea Lord at the outbreak of the 1914–18 war. He was forced to resign because of anti-German feeling. The family name was changed from Battenberg to Mountbatten at the same time as the name of the royal house was changed from Saxe-Coburg-Gotha to Windsor. Prince Louis was the father of the present Lord Mountbatten.)

In his tour of duty in *Hermes* Charles took part in exercises flying his Wessex-v helicopter which was marked with bands of brilliant orange fluorescent paint. The navy were anxious not to lose the heir to the throne while he was with them. Before the tour ended Charles managed to get a few days' holiday in the West Indies and spent them on the island of Eleuthera, staying at the villa of Lord and Lady Brabourne, who is a daughter of Lord Mountbatten. The Brabournes have five sons and two daughters, Joanna, twenty that year, and Amanda, eighteen. There has been speculation, on and off, of Charles marrying one of them. If he did, Lord Mountbatten would have truly created a dynasty, Charles being his great nephew and the bride a granddaughter.

Charles was to join the family at Balmoral for the holidays and then attend a three-month lieutenants' course in September at the Royal Naval College, Greenwich. This is a professional test in which the navy begins to sort out those who have first-class ability from those who are mediocre.

It was not easy for Charles to keep up his naval career with all the other calls on his time.

I try very hard to be as professional as possible. I hope I demonstrate a reasonable amount of enthusiasm. The difficulty is that I did a shortened course of introduction to the navy and a fairly short period of training.

I have to try that little bit harder to assimilate all the vast amount of technical information and the navigational problems rather more quickly than other people have had to do.

I think now I've managed to accustom myself to the pace and made people realize I can't necessarily live up to the programme they've mapped out.

It may well be also that Charles did not wish to immerse himself too deeply in a naval career. He was willing to do his stint and as he has said, he is not a rebel by heart, but he has become very much his own man. During his years in the navy, he made sure he kept up his outside activities.

Among his other recent activities had been a TV film, *Pilot Royal*, which was shown on BBC 2 to coincide with his twenty-seventh birthday on 14 November. It was not just about being a pilot although there was a good scene of him landing a helicopter on the top of Snowdon.

He talked about countries he had visited and said: 'They do look to Britain for an example and a lead in so many different things.' In his travels he mentioned he had noticed, as so many others working or visiting abroad, that the image of Britain created by Fleet Street and reflected in the world press, was misleading: 'You read all the papers when you're abroad and think the whole thing's coming to an end. When you come back everything is the same. Things are going on as always and you feel how marvellous it is to be back.'

In his comments he was showing a remarkable maturity. For example, he said:

I'm one of those people who believes strongly that one should always adapt to changing circumstances, particularly in my position.

The one thing you cannot afford to do is to get left miles behind. Likewise you don't want to be too far ahead. I do worry sometimes about the future. But I do think on the whole if one can preserve a sense of humour and adopt those qualities and perhaps calm things down and provide a stable appearance and a steadying influence all will be well.

Andrew had had a good year at Gordonstoun. He was shining at sports and working hard. He was determined to become a glider-pilot and in November made his first flight from Milltown Airfield in Morayshire in a two-seater. His trainer said he was quick to learn and quite fearless.

Anne had had a success at Luhmuehlen in West Germany where she was runner-up in the three-day European championships. She had not been so lucky at Burghley where she had to withdraw. By the end of the year there was some comment that Princess Anne was not expecting a baby yet. All being normal, royal marriages are usually made fruitful early. It was pointed out that in the following year, 1976, there would be another Olympic Games and Anne was probably determined to try for a place in the British team. It might be her last chance.

Soon after Davina Sheffield's return Charles renewed his friendship. He discoursed freely on love and marriage at this time in an interview given to *Woman's Own*. He said he thought that thirty would be the right sort of age to get married (that was 1978 for Charles). 'I've made sure I haven't married the first person I've fallen in love with. By this time you have seen a great deal of life, met a large number of girls, been able to see what types of girls there are, fallen in love every now and then, and you know what it's all about.' The widespread knowledge that all was not well between his aunt Princess Margaret and her husband, Lord Snowdon, gave point to his further remarks: 'Having tried to learn from other people's experiences, other people's mistakes – in one's own family and in other people's – I hope I should be able to make a reasonable decision and choice.'

At the end of the previous year, 1974, he had agreed to become president of an appeal launched by Dr Coggan, the Archbishop of Canterbury, for £3½ million to repair the fabric of the cathedral. Now Charles made a practical gesture to help. He made a thirty-minute ITV programme, which was shown early in January 1976, in which he described three aspects of the cathedral – its architecture, its history and its music. He went to Canterbury for two days' filming. Tony Maylam, the director and script-writer, described him as 'incredibly professional'. It certainly turned out one of Charles's most successful ventures into television.

In front of the tomb of the Black Prince he stood with a certain family piety and said: 'This is fascinating. He was Prince of Wales – and I am.' He handled one of the gilt and copper gauntlets and commented: 'It's a medieval form of knuckleduster – not something I'd like to meet during a battle.' He recalled the murder of Thomas à Becket, the Archbishop who was slain in the Cathedral by over-zealous knights of Henry II. Charles recited Shakespeare at the tomb of Henry IV, walked in the cloisters, attended evensong and read the lesson.

> Every time I come here, I find something new and even more beautiful which had escaped my notice before. Each time I am filled with wonder at the sheer feat of engineering that was required to create this sculptural masterpiece. The cathedral has been part of the life and heritage of this country for so many centuries now that one almost feels it is something exquisitely fashioned by nature rather than by man.

In February of the new year, 1976, Charles was given his first ship. He was to command HMS *Bronington*, a 360-ton *Tor* class minehunter which had a complement of thirty-nine. The news did not give unalloyed pleasure to Charles, as he suffers from sea-sickness. The *Bronington* is one of a class of ship that they said would roll on wet grass. She is an old ship, made of wood, sits very high out of the water and rocks a lot. On a ship of her size accommodation is cramped. Charles's cabin measured nine feet by seven. Still, it was his own ship. *Bronington* was normally based at Rosyth and Charles took her on various British and naval exercises in home waters and showed the flag in British, German and Belgian ports. Among the furniture of his cabin was a picture of Davina, delectably attired in a bikini.

March brought him two pieces of bad news.

On the eleventh Davina's mother, a widow, was found murdered in her country home near Witney in Oxfordshire. Two young men were afterwards found guilty of the murder and sentenced to life imprisonment. Charles was close enough to Davina to share her feelings of horror and sorrow.

On 19 March Buckingham Palace announced that Princess Margaret and Lord Snowdon were separating. There were two children of the marriage. Whatever personal sympathy the Queen may have had it was a blow for her that the announcement had to be made and that the press were publishing at length detailed stories of her sister's relationship with Roderick Llewellyn, a young man of twenty-eight.

Charles has said many times over the years how much his family means to him and how lucky he considers himself to be as part of a tightly knit family. Now the public scandal struck a wounding blow at this cosy family image that he had nurtured.

The Queen was fifty on 21 April. On the previous evening she gave a dinner at Windsor Castle for all the family and close friends. This was followed by a great ball for five hundred guests which went on well into the night and gave everyone the opportunity of toasting the Queen on the right day.

The same day Anne and Mark Phillips were due to take part in the Portman Horse Trials near Blandford in Dorset. Anne was riding the Queen's horse, Candlewick. In the cross-country event Mark was slightly ahead of his wife. In the last fence but one Anne's horse fell and rolled on top of her. She was unconscious when the ambulance-men arrived. Mark Phillips rushed to the scene and Anne was taken to Poole General Hospital and found to be suffering from concussion and to be very shaken. The ground was particularly hard for this was the year of the great drought in England. It seemed at first as if it was the end of Anne's Olympic hopes. Nothing could deter her, however. She was soon in the saddle again. Her determination was rewarded. She did win a place in the team. Mark Phillips would be going as reserve.

The Queen and Prince Philip were travelling to the United States of America which were celebrating the 200th anniversary of their independence. Then they were going on to Montreal to open the Games. This was another reason why Anne was so eager to be competing.

Charles had been asked earlier in the year if he would give an interview on TV in which he would have the opportunity of developing his views that his ancestor, George III, in whose reign the American colonies had rebelled, was a much maligned man and monarch. Charles agreed to do the programme after consulting his mother. The interviewer was Alastair Cooke who for so many years had entertained and informed the British nation on American affairs with charm and authority.

The programme was screened in Britain on 19 April. Charles was relaxed, confident, charming. A thoroughly professional performance. He said that history – especially American historians – had written off George III as a mad monarch and that his madness had been partly responsible for the policy which led the American colonies to revolt. Charles explained that the so-called madness was, in the light of modern medical knowledge, probably a blood disease, porphyria, which gives hallucinations and depressions. Charles added that it was hereditary. Cooke asked him if there had been any other cases in the family. 'Oh, yes, there are', replied Charles, but said no more.

He went on with great determination:

He was a complete idealist and moralist. Either a thing was right or wrong. I am determined to clear his name. It's very unfortunate if one is misunderstood in history. I personally would hate to be misunderstood.

I have a strong family feeling and so had George III. I should hate if what happened in politics should mask the King as a person, a human being who was enormously loved and respected in this country.

So far as the rebellion of the American colonies was concerned, Charles told Alastair Cooke that he thought that friction between the young America and Britain was inevitable and would have caused the break sooner or later.

Charles's interest in his ancestor has a particular significance because of his position as heir to the throne. He discoursed on the matter to Stuart Kuttner:

> ... he was a genuine, honest human being who suffered a great deal. He was a great patron of the arts, and a great patron of scientific development in the eighteenth century. I can't say I can turn round and emulate him. But I admire him enormously for what he did and for his incredible capacity for hard work and conscientious devotion to duty.

In his various comments on George III Charles does not mention the King's skilful, and for a time successful, efforts to rule through a parliamentary majority which followed him either out of loyalty or because the pay was good. Yet Charles as a student of his ancestor is obviously well aware of this political aspect of George's reign. It is, therefore, legitimate to consider to what extent Charles's attitude to politics may be influenced by George III's policy.

British Airways publishes a customers' magazine, *High Life,* which is available in all its reception areas and on its planes. It has a potential readership of millions, with a large proportion foreign. Princess Anne was interviewed by the magazine and she gave her views frankly and bluntly. She bitterly bemoaned her lot. 'We've never had a holiday. A week at Balmoral or ten days at Sandringham is the nearest we get.' She went on to say that she found sight-seeing 'purgatory'. 'You never see anything; either too many people or too many press.'

When the article was published it caused consternation in the Palace. Normally, a discreet censorship is exercised. This time her embarrassing remarks had slipped right through the safety-net. Moreover, the article, which was partially reproduced in Fleet Street, gave a very disturbing picture of Princess Anne's attitude to her position. It bore out what those who had to meet her at various functions had noticed – but kept to a small circle – she was at times surly, uninterested and perilously near to being downright rude.

Soon after this it was announced that the Queen had bought Gatcombe Park, a 730-acre estate in the Cotswolds for Princess Anne and Mark Phillips. It had belonged to Lord Butler, Master of Trinity, Cambridge, Charles's college. Lord Butler, who did not come from a notably wealthy family, had married the heiress daughter of Samuel Courtauld, the textile manufacturer. The estate, which cost around £700,000, contained a delightful mansion, considerable stabling, 530 acres of farmland, 200 acres of woodland and a half share in a lake which has brown trout.

The estate lies in the Beaufort Hunt country, is ten miles from Badminton, seat of the Horse Trials, and a few miles from Captain Phillips's birthplace, Tetbury.

In announcing the news at this particular time the Queen seemed to show a rare failing in predicting public reaction. There was a slight raising of eyebrows in even the most loyal circles. Some Labour MPs naturally made more of it than that.

Mr Ronald Thomas MP said: 'In the economic crisis, when working people are having to take considerable cuts in their standard of living, I find this example of the flaunting of wealth appalling and, indeed, obscene.'

Several Labour MPs tabled a Commons' motion saying the provision of fifty houses for families in need would have been a much more worthy investment.

It was said the Queen had been to a certain extent driven to provide the estate for her daughter. Anne was developing such an aversion to public duties that she might give it all up and virtually retire. This would make it very difficult for the Queen to expect Parliament to provide for her out of public funds. The estate, well-farmed, could provide her and her husband with an adequate income.

Charles found that his duties commanding HMS *Bronington* were not too onerous. He was able to play a good deal of polo this summer at Windsor and elsewhere. He was often with Davina Sheffield. In June he invited her to Windsor for a carriage horse event on Smith's Lawn. She also went there to watch Charles playing polo and sat in the royal box with the Queen and Prince Philip.

This season, however, may well have been Davina's swan-song. By September she was saying in words that seemed to ring true that she had not seen Charles for three months. Certainly she had not been seen with him in public or semi-public events.

Talking to the *Daily Mirror* in September about her relations with Charles she said, 'It is a private matter to me although I have no doubt people might regard it as public ... I have seen reports in the newspapers about the Prince and myself but can say nothing.' The *Daily Mail* and other newspapers, however, were still forecasting at this time that Charles would marry Davina.

It may be that this summer the Queen decided Davina's life-style could harm the royal image. The break-up of Princess Margaret's marriage earlier in the year had already dealt it a blow.

It is almost impossible to imagine the Queen agreeing to Charles marrying Davina. Of course, Charles may never have had any intention of marrying her and the press may have made wrong assumptions. They might well have been based on the somewhat old-fashioned belief that if a young man of Charles's position took his girl-friend to meet his parents on several occasions he was thinking of her seriously.

The Queen, accompanied by Prince Philip, opened the Olympic Games on 17 July. Charles, Andrew and Edward were all there to see Anne competing. For her the odds were very high.

Well over ten years ago, she had set her sights on reaching the top as a horsewoman. Finally, she had made the grade and was a member of Britain's Olympic team. At Montreal she would be competing against the best of the world. Her family were watching. Through TV and the press the world was watching. If she succeeded the world would applaud and if she failed ...

She was riding Goodwill, who had been trained to perfection. The cross-country run was a difficult course with thirty-six fences. She was nearly half-way round when she fell. She lay dazed and bruised on the ground for several minutes. Then she got up, remounted and made her way over the remaining fences. She showed great courage. But the faults incurred put her out of the running. It was not a good year for the British team. It was the end of a chapter. For Anne would be twenty-six this year and was expected to start having a family soon.

At this time *The Times* published a powerful leading article suggesting that Prince Charles should be considered seriously by the Australians as their next Governor-General. There had been talk about it from time to time over the last three years in a vague way. The thinking behind it was that Charles would probably soon be leaving the navy and would need, and deserved, a job to match his ability.

The Times now gave its weight to the idea because a constitutional crisis had occurred there in November 1975. It had directly involved the Queen's representative, the Governor-General, Sir John Kerr. He had dismissed the Prime Minister, Mr Whitlam, and his Labour government, and called a general election which resulted in a considerable victory for the Conservative party led by Mr Fraser. Since then such strong feelings had been expressed by Mr Whitlam and his supporters that the standing of the monarchy in Australia had been adversely affected. 'It seems, to outsiders,' said *The Times*, 'that Australia needs to wipe the slate clean as soon as possible. The Labour Party has ensured that this cannot be done until a new Governor-General can be appointed.' In putting forward Prince Charles as a possible solution to the problem *The Times* commented: 'He would have to be, so to speak, a full-time Australian during the appointment, and so his duties in Britain would have to be moved to other shoulders. That is perfectly feasible. But everything depends on Australian feelings which naturally cannot be fully measured in Britain – Britain can only agree to spare the Prince.'

The kite flown by *The Times* had a mixed reception in Australia. Prince Charles is very popular there, but it has been taken for granted for some time that the governor-generals should be Australians (as is Sir John Kerr).

There the matter rested for the time being.

Just before Andrew went to the Olympic Games he completed three solo circuits in a glider and qualified for his Cadet Corps glider proficiency wings. He was playing cricket in the First Eleven this summer and was fast becoming a good all-rounder. He also passed his 0-levels without trouble.

In an exchange visit he was one of a party of fifteen Gordonstoun boys which went for three weeks to the Caousou Jesuit College near Toulouse. On arriving he said to reporters: 'My name is Andrew Edwards. My father is a gentleman farmer and my mother does not work.' The last remark was very much in Andrew's vein of mocking humour. He stayed with a local doctor, played against a French football team and did some sight-seeing. When the visit was over one of the local teachers said: '*Mon Dieu!* He certainly was a handful.'

Prince Charles was to leave the navy on 14 December. He had spent about five years in the service and commented: 'There are other things to do and it would be rather selfish of me if I remained locked away here.' In November he brought the *Bronington* up the Thames to the Tower Basin. Prince Andrew was aboard and the press were invited to have a look round.

On the day he left the service he was given a hearty farewell by his shipmates. He was pushed ashore in a wheelchair, with a lavatory seat and festoons of toilet paper round his neck. From the sick bay 'Doc' Ryan's parting advice was, 'Keep your bowels open!' The press reports and pictures did not please some of the senior officers in the Admiralty. But the *Bronington* was a young man's ship and the tone of the farewell reflected the way Charles had tried to overcome the difficult task of being accepted as 'one of them'. It was Charles's style.

He had earlier expressed his views on management: 'One of the most important things is to be as honest and genuine as possible. People can always see through you if you are being artificial – particularly a sailor. But the most important thing about a position of responsibility or command is to get a chap to do something willingly.'

At the end of the year Charles followed his sister in having an interview with the British Airways magazine, *High Life*. His remarks were more positive:

'Britain has indulged in far more self-indignation than is good for her. There are millions of people who work incredibly hard and achieve magnificent things without any recognition whatever.'

But he also had a light touch:

'I enjoy speaking French, particularly with a beautiful French lady and after a glass of something.'

To end off Charles's year he was promoted commander in the Royal Navy and a wing-commander in the RAF.

In January 1977 Andrew went to Canada to spend six months at Lakefield College in the Kawartha Lake District about seventy miles east of Toronto. Charles's time at Timbertop in Australia had been a success so that it seemed sensible for Andrew to spend some time in a Commonwealth country. Mr Pierre Trudeau, the Canadian Prime Minister, gave his approval. Andrew was keen from the start and was looking forward to the ice-hockey, ski-ing and canoeing. It was just his sort of world. Apart from Andrew's feelings, however, was the need to involve Commonwealth countries with the life of a new generation of the royal family.

Lakeside draws its pupils from well-to-do families, but claims to be 'sensitive and responsive to the changing needs of Canadian society', which means that in Canada economic democracy is likely to follow political democracy.

Lakeside has an exchange programme with Gordonstoun and shares some of its attitudes. When Andrew arrived he met the boy who was to replace him at Gordonstoun. He could not let the opportunity pass. He warned him: 'The beds are as hard as iron. It's straw mattresses and bread and water. It's just like a prison!'

After three weeks at Lakeside Andrew commented: 'The school is quite excellent and so are the facilities. But it's not just that – the boys here are terrific. They are different from chaps in England because they have a different outlook from a different country.'

The year 1977 marked the Silver Jubilee of the Queen's reign and she and Prince Philip visited New Zealand and Australia on the first of their many celebration tours. In Australia she had a great welcome, which was reassuring after the fears that the constitutional crisis had diminished the monarchy's popularity. The Queen discussed with the Australian Prime Minister and others the suggestion that Charles should go there as Governor-General. The London *Evening Standard* carried on 6 March a report which bore the signs of being authoritative. It said that the appointment of Charles was ruled out, adding that the Queen had decided there was 'no such possibility both for personal and political reasons. Charles was too young and inexperienced.' The Queen wanted him to marry first and be well settled before taking on added responsibilities.

Charles at the time was visiting several African members of the Commonwealth, mixing formal and informal events. Ghana impressed him. He said that he had experienced there 'this strange Commonwealth feeling, which so often seems to endure despite the difficulties of the past and the uncertainties of the future. I can only describe the feeling as being, as it were, "at home".'

After this tour Charles took a ten-day holiday to the West Indies. He went to the island of Eleuthera once more to stay with Lord and Lady Brabourne and some of their children.

On Good Friday, 8 April, it was announced that Princess Anne was expecting a baby in November. She and her husband were moving into their new home, Gatcombe Park in the Cotswolds, in the late summer. The house had been extensively and expensively repaired and redecorated.

To mark the Queen's Silver Jubilee there was to be an appeal for money to finance youth projects. This was tailor-made for Charles. He had been thinking and talking for years about the need to inspire young people to help in community projects. He was made chairman and made a national appeal on TV on Sunday 24 April, from his new home at Chevening, which looked during the programme like a film set of an English aristocrat's country home – everything right, nothing out of place and completely lacking an impress of his own personality.

He said:

The Silver Jubilee Trust will use its money, quite simply, to help young people to help others. [Its purpose would be] to encourage work in hospitals and homes, help for the elderly and disabled or mentally handicapped, for deprived and sick children, work to improve the local environment, rescue services, adventure projects and other forms of leadership training ... Since the Queen is head of the Commonwealth some of the schemes it will support will also involve the young from other Commonwealth countries.

Three years before he had said:

I'm old enough, and I've seen enough to worry about the alienation of young people from adult society. Mainly in London and the big cities; I don't think it's so tough in the country towns and villages. I think what's wrong is that so many young people feel they don't belong, because they don't have a sense of being useful, of being of service, of contributing. In the cities, the young coloured people feel this even more strongly.

Charles developed the theme:

Because they feel like this, young people burst out from time to time in aggression. What they really want is adventure and a sense of service, and if they can't have the combination, they'll go for the adventure, even if it means wrongdoing, anti-social behaviour, violence. It's a problem that's always been with us, but more noticeably since the end of national service.

He realizes that young people don't want to be told what to do by the Establishment – 'they feel they are remote, irrelevant.' He sees the answer in young people running their own show. 'They don't want to do things which are prescribed, planned and supervised by adults.'

He told Kenneth Harris with whom he was talking at the time that he realized these projects would need finance.

> I believe it is possible to find the funds required. The central idea is this: there would be a trust holding the funds. Young people, including existing organizations, would come to the trust and say, 'We want to do this. Will you give us the money?' The trust could then examine the proposals; if they thought they would work, they would say: 'Right; there's the money, and any help we can give. Get on with it.'

His ideas, he admitted, owed much to the Gordonstoun philosophy created by Kurt Hahn. So that although Charles had not been happy at the school, in the long run Hahn had won. The ideas also owed a lot to his father, Prince Philip, another Hahn product, who had also tried through the Duke of Edinburgh's Award Scheme to tackle the problem.

Jubilee or not, Charles was being married off again by Fleet Street. This time it was to Princess Marie-Astrid of Luxembourg, an attractive girl of twenty-three, who was studying English literature at a language school in Cambridge. She is the daughter of the Grand Duke of Luxembourg and granddaughter of the former King Leopold and Queen Astrid of the Belgians. Marie-Astrid is a Roman Catholic and this would, unless contentious legislation was introduced, debar any possibility of her marrying the heir to the British throne. This did not stop the rumours. Charles was said to have known the Princess for over a year.

At the beginning of May Charles spoke at the annual dinner of the Newspaper Society and decided to talk about these marriage rumours and press sensationalism generally.

He said that a few years ago he had been 'rash enough' to say when interviewed by a woman's magazine that he thought thirty was a reasonable age for a man to get married. 'Since then I seem to have been married off to many ladies of indeterminate origin.'

He went on to say that he understood the difficulties the press faced in establishing the truth of the stories they receive and that he realized the economic pressures to sensationalize news.

'Nevertheless when all is said and done what is really needed is a sense of proportion, something which Britain always seems to have retained.'

A few weeks later Charles was given an opportunity to assess the impact of his speech. On Friday 17 June, the *Daily Express* carried a report stating positively that on the following Monday an announcement would be made of his engagement to Marie-Astrid. It is customary practice in Fleet Street, however well-authenticated such a story may seem, to make certain reservations: 'We have it on good authority'; 'It now seems almost certain that'; 'Unless last minute changes are made', and so on. But this time the *Express* hedged no bets.

When the first edition of the *Daily Express* appeared around midnight in the other offices of Fleet Street, there was frantic activity. The professionals were sure that the *Express* would never have been so positive without very good reasons indeed. Buckingham Palace officials had a disturbed night. So did Prince Charles.

Finally, during the early hours, an official denial was issued: 'There are no plans for an announcement of Prince Charles's engagement on Monday or at any other time. He has either never met Princess Marie-Astrid, or, if he has, it has been no more than a formal handshake at official functions.'

Even this firm denial left lingering doubts in Fleet Street. As Charles knew – he had commented on the fact – journalists found it difficult to believe any royal denial about marriage after Princess Anne and Mark Phillips had asserted positively in March 1973 that there was no truth in the rumours they were to marry, only to announce their engagement on 29 May.

During Friday a spokesman for the Grand Duke of Luxembourg issued a denial that his daughter was about to be engaged to Charles. The Grand Duke had a few days earlier announced that he was giving a press reception on the following Monday. He does not give many press receptions. It may have been this that induced the *Daily Express* to throw caution to the wind.

The *Daily Mirror* kept the marriage story going on the Saturday in an article by Audrey Whiting who has written for many years on the royal family. She said: 'Two weeks ago in the *Sunday Mirror* I broke the news that people close to the Queen held strong views that an engagement is in the offing this year – possibly to be announced about the time of his twenty-ninth birthday in November.' Audrey Whiting had carefully hedged her bets.

During the summer of 1977 Charles's guest for polo at Windsor and at other social occasions had been Lady Sarah Spencer, twenty-two, the eldest of three daughters of Earl Spencer. In escorting Lady Sarah, Charles was back in the same circle as that of Lady Jane Wellesley. The Spencers are descended from John Spencer, son of the third Earl of Sunderland, who married Anne Churchill, daughter and co-heir of the great Duke of Marlborough. They have since been one of the great establishment families, landowners, statesmen and art collectors. They have always been close to the court – the men Knights of the Garter, the women Ladies of the Bedchamber. The Spencers are the leading family of Northamptonshire where they own the great house of Althrop.

With Lady Jane, descendant of the great Duke of Wellington, and Lady Sarah, descendant of the Great Duke of Marlborough, Prince Charles has made friends of girls sprung from the two greatest soldiers in British history, who both also played an important political role. Probably, however, the sense of history which he possesses has not been uppermost in his mind.

At the service in St Paul's on 7 June to mark the Silver Jubilee, all the Queen's children were present to take part in the national thanksgiving for her twenty-five years of service on the throne.

The Jubilee Day had a success beyond all expectations. *The Times* next morning carried the headline across its front page: 'One million people greet the Queen on her Silver Jubilee Day.'

Her children could be proud of their mother. They could also consider the dedication she had shown for twenty-five years to earn the tributes. There was a lesson.

Princess Anne and her husband soon after went on a five-day visit to the United States. She was to unveil a statue of Queen Anne at Centreville, Queen Anne's County, Maryland, but she also attended the Jubilee garden party at the British Embassy in Washington, lunched with Mr Carter's son and his wife in the White House, and had a ten-minute meeting with the President.

Princess Anne was aware of the unfavourable impression she had left behind her in Washington after her visit with Charles in 1970. This time she took trouble to be most charming and won golden opinions.

Both Charles and Andrew were in Canada during July. Andrew, after his terms at Lakeside, had before him a ten-day adventure holiday in northern Canada. The headmaster, Mr Terry Guest, took him and four Canadian schoolfriends on the trip. A picture arrived of him looking tough and happy as he started off in a canoe – in the lead position – on the 280-mile trip down the Coppermine River to the Arctic Ocean.

Charles visited the Indian tribes in Southern Alberta which were celebrating the centenary of their treaties with the original white settlers. He rode with the chief of the Blackfoot tribe and was made an honorary chief of the Blood tribe in an elaborate initiation which included adorning his face with sacred paint and taking part in ritual dances.

When he came back at the end of the month, Prince Charles had a happy return to Aberystwyth. He was installed as Chancellor of the University and given an honorary degree of music because he is 'reputed to be a very good cello player'. There was a touch of Welsh mockery in this, as he has said himself that his skill as a cellist has been much exaggerated. There was also a touch of Welsh admiration. They admired his courage in going to Aberystwyth at a time when there was much violent talk and some violent action directed against him.

In August Andrew and Edward sailed in the royal yacht

with the Queen and Prince Philip to troubled Ulster. It was the most difficult of the Jubilee tours and security arrangements were very strict. Andrew attended a Youth Festival of 1,800 young people and looked as if he was thoroughly enjoying himself. He helped to create a relaxed atmosphere in a situation not without its tenseness.

Charles was developing his ideas about the Commonwealth. He told some young students, 'I do not think it would be a disaster if Britain withdrew from the Commonwealth. I am sure it could survive without Britain.' He went on to say that Britain represented the centre of the Commonwealth only because the Queen, as Head of the Commonwealth, resided in London.

Charles is probably thinking, like others, that it might be well for the future if the offices of the Commonwealth were in another area, for example, the Caribbean.

On 21 September he flew to the aircraft carrier, *Ark Royal*, and took his place in the observer's seat of a Phantom supersonic fighter which then was catapulted from the flight-deck. The *Ark Royal* was the last ship in the navy to have catapults and Charles, in spite of some misgivings at the Palace, wanted to see what it was like. This was shortly after he had told a group of young journalists at Windsor, 'I believe in living life dangerously and I think a lot of others do as well. I believe in challenge and adventure and working as a team for some particular aim can do a great deal of good.'

Andrew, enlivened by his six months in Canada earlier in the year, went back to Gordonstoun to study for his A-levels which he was to take in 1979. Edward went with him to start his years at the school.

Both Charles and Andrew showed paintings at an exhibition in Windsor Castle at the beginning of October. The show, 'Royal Performance', was part of the Windsor Festival and consisted of 50 works of art by past and present members of the royal family. Prince Philip had already shown his work at a small exhibition at the Royal Academy.

Charles has been painting for some years. He took up watercolours which he found 'very difficult, but most rewarding'. The art critic of the *Sunday Telegraph*, Michael Shepherd, said of his work in the Windsor exhibition that it 'reveals a promising artistic personality of boldness combined with sensitivity, and subtle sense of colour.'

He continued: 'More surprising, though less skilled as yet, Prince Andrew, in one of his Canadian landscape paintings ... shows an adventurous sense of abstraction and composition beyond the usual admirable amateurism of royal performers.'

In the autumn Charles went to the United States and Australia in a tour designed to widen his experience and to do good for the monarchy. For many visitors – including the privileged – knowledge of the United States is confined to Washington and New York. For Charles a tour was arranged which enabled him to see something of the variety and extent of the country. He went to the mid-West—Chicago and Cleveland—to the Far-West—Los Angeles and San Francisco—to the South—St Louis, Atlanta and Charleston—and on to Texas to the now legendary oil and space city of Houston. It showed once more how privileged he is for such a visit would be the dream, unlikely to be realized, of every young man or woman. What is more, everywhere there were knowledgeable people to show him around. In Chicago, that tough, proud city with one of the best art galleries in the world, the local press gave him headlines as 'Charles The Charming', and at a banquet he said, 'I must have shaken about a thousand hands, and I also received numerous, delicious Chicago kisses'. He spoke to a gathering of the students at the university and when asked what he considered the value of monarchy to be replied: 'In a way, it fills a certain need or desire some people have ... I think its greatest advantage is that it's human, above politics.'

The remark. 'it fills a certain need or desire some people have', is significant. It showed that Charles has rationalized his task to his own satisfaction. Many of the ceremonial occasions, in various uniforms, which it will be his life-long job to perform, could well be irksome to an intelligent man such as Charles. But, if he sees himself as satisfying needs or desires that society, perhaps irrationally, wants to be satisfied, then the formal visits, the dressing-up, the ritual gestures have some meaning. What is more, Charles is enough of an actor to take pleasure in the drama.

He flew on to Australia where he is always sure of a great welcome after his Timbertop days. He met Mr Fraser, the Prime Minister, attended a gala concert in the Sydney Opera House and launched a pop-music record album all in aid of the Silver Jubilee Appeal for young Australians. Just before he left he visited Alice Springs and attended a splendid lunch which unfortunately gave him a touch of food poisoning on his flight home. Twenty other guests and three of the staff were also taken ill so that the journey was a white-faced affair.

On his return home he spent a day in bed, but was well enough to travel to Yorkshire to stay with Lord Halifax, a local grandee and friend of the family. He had his 29th birthday there on 14 November and celebrated the day by going fox-hunting with the local Middleton Hunt.

Charles, however, like the rest of his family, was waiting for news of Anne's baby which was expected at any time now. She had hoped in her determined way that the event would take place on 14 November for it would be the fourth anniversary of her marriage and the birthday of Charles. But her boy arrived a few hours late, just before 11 a.m. on Tuesday, 15 November.

Although the family would disclaim any belief in the occult powers and influence of astrology, it does seem that the Queen favours mid-November as an auspicious time for herself and her children. She was married on 20 November; Charles was born on 14 November; Anne was married on 14 November and her son arrived on 15 November. The days all fall under the sign of Scorpio which runs from 24 October to 22 November. It might be a shrewd bet that Charles when he marries will choose a date around 14 November.

Anne had her baby in St Mary's Hospital, Paddington, in the presence of Mark Phillips with Mr George Pinker, the Queen's gynaecologist in attendance. It had previously been announced that no title would be given by the Queen so that

Master Phillips became the first royal child to be born a commoner for more than five hundred years.

A 21-gun salute was fired at the Tower of London by the Honourable Artillery Company. The customary salute by the King's Troop, Royal Horse Artillery, in Hyde Park, was not fired for a contemporary reason. The men were on stand-by duty to replace firemen who were on strike.

The Prime Minister, Mr Callaghan, however, sent the traditional message of congratulation from the House of Commons and a flag was hoisted and church bells rung in the village of Great Somerford in Wiltshire where Mark Phillips's parents live. The Queen, looking very happy, went to see her first grandchild in the evening and two days later Anne left hospital with the baby.

On 22 December the boy was christened Peter Mark Andrew by the Archbishop of Canterbury in the Music Room at Buckingham Palace. Peter is the first name of Captain Phillips's father and Mark his own name. Andrew, apart from being the name of Anne's second brother, has many links with the Greek Royal family of which Prince Philip was a member.

The godparents were interestingly varied. There were Prince Charles and the Rt Rev Geoffrey Tiarks, a cousin of Mark Phillips on his mother's side, who was Bishop of Maidstone before his retirement. Captain Hamish Lochore was a friend of Mark and Mrs Timothy Holderness-Roddam was a friend of both Anne and Mark, for as Jane Bullen she had been a noted horsewoman.

The status of Anne and Mark Phillips as landowners had been strengthened shortly before the birth of their son. The Queen bought for them another estate adjoining Gatcombe Park. It is Aston Farm, Cherington, covers 600 acres and cost around £250,000. With Gatcombe Park the Phillips now own around 1,200 acres which had been bought for about a million pounds. The farms grow wheat and barley and there are beef and dairy herds.

To round off the emergence of Mark Phillips as a landowner it was announced that he would be leaving the army in 1978 and taking a year's course in farming at the Royal Agricultural College at Cirencester. It was an appropriate step for there was not much future for him in the army after his marriage. He was barred from doing service in Northern Ireland or any other trouble spot so that his chances of promotion were negligible unless by royal patronage and this was thought inappropriate. The acquisition of a country estate, remote from people, especially the press, was a comfort for Princess Anne. Soon her husband would be relieved of his duties in the army, trained as a farmer, and able to devote himself to the management of the estate. They could be seen as steps in the creation of the private life for which the Princess yearns.

Towards the end of the year there was a slight scandal at Gordonstoun where Prince Andrew and Prince Edward were back for the autumn term. Five boys and a girl were expelled after cannabis had been found. One of the boys was Constantine Niarchos, the 15-year-old son of Mr Stavros Niarchos, the Greek shipping tycoon. The boy, it is said, will inherit £40m when he is 21. It was a blow for the prestige of the Niarchos family. But prestige was kept up in another fashion. A private jet was sent to pick up the boy at the Lossiemouth RAF base.

His expulsion could be described as – jet-propelled.

11
Charles Shows His Mettle

The customary family holiday at Sandringham in January, with its round of riding and shooting, was enlivened for Prince Andrew by a girl-friend, Kirsty Richmond, who came to stay for a few days. She is also at Gordonstoun, aged seventeen, and a well-built, attractive girl, who is the daughter of Mrs Vaurie Richmond, a school nurse living in the Suffolk village of Great Barton, near Bury St Edmunds. She is a widow and has made sacrifices to send Kirsty to Gordonstoun. It has been worthwhile for Kirsty has done well and took her A-levels in 1978.

Before he went back to school Andrew had a few days in London and went out on the town one evening, ending up at the fashionable Annabel's with a group of friends. Andrew, in his nonchalant style, arrived without a tie, a deficiency the club swiftly made up. His partner for the evening was Julia Guinness, eighteen, whose family name needs no introduction.

Andrew was now familiarly known as 'Randy Andy', a nickname acquired in Canada where his Robert Redford looks had not lacked admirers.

During this term at school Andrew had his eighteenth birthday, 19 February, and became entitled to £20,000 a year from the Civil List. But this did not mean he was going to get it, as he somewhat ruefully admitted. The Queen made arrangements for most of it to be invested until he has finished his education. He will be given £600 p.a.

Charles had soon broken off his family visit to Sandringham and gone ski-ing for a fortnight at Klosters in Switzerland with some friends, among whom was the now almost inevitable Lady Sarah Spencer.

He came back to get ready for an important visit to Brazil and Venezuela which was to take up most of March. The visit was important for it was a forerunner of the tours he will be making in the future, taking off some of the burden from his mother and father. Apart from general goodwill, royal tours have these days a certain relevance to our export trade. Brazil, an emerging giant, had in the past many German immigrants who have done well in business and tend to favour West Germany. Japan has also made great strides in the area. Venezuela, rich in oil, has become closely linked with the United States for both imports and exports. So Charles faced a challenge.

He faced a heavy programme and he completed it with great zest, often piloting one of the aircraft of the Queen's Flight which had been sent over to help him cover the great distances. In Rio he was quite like his father in his younger days, lecturing the British Chamber of Commerce on the need to do more to match German and Japanese enterprise. Such royal lectures do not tend to go down well, as his father discovered. It is dangerous for any visitor of a few days to tell men how to do their job – and is not appreciated.

Charles's youthful enthusiasm inspired the *Daily Express* to print a story that he had been offered £50,000 a year by a group of British businessmen to tour the world on behalf of the export trade. Charles reacted very angrily, presumably considering it cheapened his position.

He fitted in some sport and pleasure during the tour. He played polo, danced an abandoned samba in Rio and at Sao Paolo told the Governor with whom he was dining that he would like to finish off the evening at a night-club. Brazilian Governors are men of power. The most fashionable place, the Hippopotamus, was cleared of the public and Charles with some of his staff and a group of Brazilian officials went off to enjoy a few uninhibited hours with the help of some beautiful coffee-coloured girls.

In Venezuela Charles tried to interest its President in a

scheme near to his heart – the United World Colleges which are a development of the ideals of Kurt Hahn, the founder of Gordonstoun. This year Charles has taken over the presidency from Lord Mountbatten. The founding college is at St Donat's Castle in Wales and now there are offshoots in Singapore and on Vancouver Island, Canada.

The young men and women spend two pre-university years at the colleges, often studying for the International Baccalauréat, and taking part in social and community work. The students are generally sponsored by governments or large companies and are chosen on merit regardless of colour or background. Its admirers see it as a practical programme to produce a cadre of young men and women who will influence the world for good. Others view it as another tentacle in the octopus spread of the Gordonstoun mafia.

Charles told the President of Venezuela of the need there was to set up a new U.W.C. College where the students, taught by experts, would learn how to produce food on a cheaper and wider scale. The President did respond by setting up a feasibility study and Charles is keeping in touch, to see what the results are – just as he is pushing ahead the formation of another College in the Trieste area to serve Europe. Charles envisages the development of U.W.C. as a major personal interest in the years ahead which will enable him to visit countries not just as a royal dignitary but as a man trying to get things done which will help the world of the future.

During the Easter holidays in April Andrew appeared with another girl-friend – an attractive seventeen-year-old brunette, Clio Nathaniels, who was also at Gordonstoun. She is the daughter of an architect who went with his wife to live in the Bahamas after the war. Clio was invited to spend a week-end at Windsor and went with Andrew, Charles and Sarah Spencer to a horse-jumping event of the North Warwickshire Hunt at Hatton, near Warwick. At Gordonstoun the girls said in their sprightly, slightly bitchy way that Clio had joined 'Andrew's harem'.

A few days later both brothers faced sterner tasks and went on a parachute course. Charles had dropped by parachute into the sea during his training with the RAF, but he had since been appointed Colonel-in-Chief of The Parachute Regiment and wanted to be able to put up his parachute badge so that he could feel he was really part of the unit. As for Andrew, well, he just wanted his badge to add to his glider proficiency one already earned in the Air Training Corps. After the customary drops from a balloon, Andrew was to jump from a Hercules aircraft flying at 1,000 feet in Gloucestershire. Television cameras and press photographers were there and were able to record some drama. The canopy of the parachute opened, but the lines became entangled and Andrew had to spin round seven times to get them straight. However, he made a safe landing and went on to complete the course, commenting, 'Of course I was nervous. If you're not nervous you'll do something stupid.' He received his insignia and a certificate from Air Marshal Sir Alfred Ball and looked proud and happy – rightly so. Charles completed his course with less drama and got his badge.

Charles gave a press conference at Buckingham Palace on 4 May to announce the final result of the Queen's Silver Jubilee Appeal of which he is chairman. It had raised £16 m, more than any other public appeal before it – and, even allowing for inflation, it was a remarkable tribute to the Queen who, the Prince said, had been deeply touched by the response. The money will be spent to help young people to work to help others of all ages in the community and the Commonwealth. Among the projects already approved have been helping apprentices in Northern Ireland to rebuild an old minibus for community service and paying sixth-formers in Ayr and Arran to tape-record local newspapers for the blind. There have been criticisms – sometimes of the projects, sometimes that projects are being turned down. But that is inevitable. You cannot please everyone and Charles is taking a close and continuing interest to see that the money is spent well. Looking after the trust funds that have been formed has become part of his business life.

So far this year, 1978, you could say that Charles had had a busy, interesting time with no drama to focus the attention of Britain and the world on him. But now all this was to change. For the rest of the year he was the centre not just of interest, but often to open controversy.

It started from the fact that Charles would be thirty on 14 November. That age does mark in most men's lives the end of the formative years. From then on a man is no longer considered young, but as a mature person responsible for what he says and does. But, in addition, Charles was still unmarried and it had not been forgotten that in 1975 Charles had told a woman's magazine that he thought thirty would be the right sort of age to marry.

On May 15 the powerful American news magazine, *Time*, started the ball rolling. It made Charles its cover-story and obtained a very revealing interview with an anonymous 'intimate of three generations of the family' whom many considered must have been Lord Mountbatten. If that was so it was a journalist coup for Mountbatten is the elder statesman of the family and has had, as Charles admits, a great influence on him, particularly since he has grown up.

'I'll give you a prophecy,' said Anon in the article, 'Charles won't marry for some time yet. If I were a betting man, I'd put very heavy odds that there's not the remotest chance of his getting engaged for at least a year, and more probably two. It's certainly not going to be any of the girls mentioned in the press so far.

'Charles knows the sort of girl he wants to marry, but I would not think he's sure that he's actually met "the one". He does not want anyone who is likely to accept him very readily. If she did, it would be for the wrong reason – wanting to be Queen. The girl he's searching for is the one who does not want to be Queen, who will only do it out of love for him and affectionately desire to help and serve him. Those whom he goes about with are the ones he is not going to marry, and one day a girl will appear of whom the press has probably never heard.'

Anon then went on to attack 'the bloody press', I think unfairly, for wrecking Charles's romance with Lady Jane Wellesley. 'She would have been right for Queen and Charles's wife, but she was never given a chance by the press, and now there's no likelihood of it happening. Charles has learned his lesson. He's never going to expose the girl he hopes to win over to the press.'

Then Anon went on to discuss the sort of girl Charles might choose: 'There is not the least objection to a girl from the U.S. or the Commonwealth, but I think it's very unlikely . . . As for foreign princesses let's put it this way. There are, for one reason or another, no truly suitable candidates around. Princess Marie-Astrid of Luxemburg, whom Charles has hardly met, is most suitable, but this was never really on. Charles is prohibited by law from marrying a Roman Catholic . . . Nor do I think Charles will marry a German princess . . . I think Charles will prefer to go for an English girl as his Queen because it will make no difficulties regarding the country's acceptance. Nonetheless, there are problems that have to be overcome even in the case of a nice English girl who fulfils all the personal requirements.

'Firstly, the girl's family has got to be thought about. Because if the girl is going to be Queen of England, you can't altogether push her family aside. It's got to be a family that fits. It hasn't got to be aristocratic. It's got to be nice – that's all. The girl doesn't have to have a title. She can be Miss Something-or-Other, provided she's suitable as a wife and Queen.'

Anon finished his remarks on the subject with this judgment: 'A *coup de foudre* – this falling in love at first sight – is not the way that royal marriages are made. They invariably require growing together, mutual affection, trust, love, the desire to be together and have children. That is the way Charles looks at it, I know. He has got to know her frightfully well. It's one thing to pop into bed with a pretty girl. It's another to make your life with her.'

On May 18 the Treasury gave details of the sums to be paid to the royal family from the Civil List during 1978. This had become an annual revision since Mr (later Sir) Harold Wilson, then Prime Minister, had piloted through Parliament the Civil List Act in 1975 to ensure that the royal family was basically insulated from inflation. The main interest this time was on the allocation to Princess Margaret, whose life-style in recent years had come under criticism. She was given an increase from £55,000 to £59,000 p.a. which provoked even more comment so that scarcely a word was said about the other increases. Princess Anne's allocation was raised from £50,000 to £60,000 p.a. and it was said that the increase was largely due to the installation of security precautions at the Princess's new home, Gatcombe Park. The necessary provision was made for Andrew's £20,000 p.a. Edward, who had had his fourteenth birthday on 10 March, will have to wait another four years before he becomes eligible for his £20,000 p.a.

Prince Charles does not appear in the Civil List. As Prince of Wales he receives the revenues of the Duchy of Cornwall. They had been running at the rate of around £220,000 p.a. of which a half is contributed to the Treasury. This year, however, partly due to inflation, partly to good management, the revenues had increased to £290,000 of which Charles keeps half, £145,000.

The entire royal family is money-conscious. The Queen is prudent by nature. Prince Philip keeps a close eye on expenditure – perhaps not so surprisingly for until his marriage he had to watch his pennies – old pennies at that.

However, the increases for the royal family went through smoothly. June arrived with the Trooping the Colour on the Queen's official birthday, the ritual of royal Ascot and the other traditional pleasures of the summer, and then suddenly Prince Charles exposed to the world what Clifford Longley, the religious affairs correspondent of *The Times*, called, 'The Time-Bomb Under The Throne'. After a speech he made to the Salvation Army's International Congress at the Empire Pool, Wembley on Friday, 30 June, Charles was at the centre of a controversy about marriage which involved members of his family, his own rights of succession to the Throne, the Church of England and the Papacy.

The origin of the matter was the desire of Prince Michael of Kent, thirty-five, younger brother of the Duke of Kent, to

marry Mrs Marie-Christine Troubridge, thirty-three, a Roman
Catholic, whom he had known for some time. She had been
born Baroness Marie-Christine von Reibnitz and had married
Mr Thomas Troubridge, a banker, in 1971. The marriage ran
into difficulties and was finally annulled with the help and
advice of a Roman Catholic priest in London. Under the terms
of the Act of Settlement of 1701, Prince Michael, sixteenth in
line to the throne, would automatically lose any rights to succession by marrying a Roman Catholic. There was never any
doubt about that.

The problem facing Prince Michael and Marie-Christine
was how to get married. It proved remarkably difficult.

Prince Michael is a member of the Church of England of
which the Queen is Supreme Governor. It does not allow
second marriages to be celebrated in church. Some Anglican
clergy have in the past exercised their right under the civil law
to remarry divorcees, but this solution, if a clergyman could
have been found, was considered too much 'Hole-in-the-corner'
for a royal prince. So, towards the end of February Prince
Michael and Marie-Christine went to see the Archbishop of
Canterbury, Dr Coggan, to seek his help.

In the canon law of the Roman Church a marriage which has
been officially annulled according to its rules is as if it had never
happened. But the Church of England has no truck with this
procedure. If a person has been married, he or she has been
married and nothing can alter the fact. Dr Coggan was unable
to help.

It might have been thought at this stage that an easy solution was to marry in a registry office. Unfortunately, there are
no provisions in English law to enable a member of the royal
family to make such a marriage in England or Wales.

It was then decided to approach the Church of Rome. Marie-
Christine's marriage having been annulled there was a possibility she could be married in a Roman Catholic Church. Prince
Michael is an Anglican but the Church of Rome allows mixed
marriages to be celebrated, with certain safeguards.

Marie-Christine's family came from Vienna and the hope
was that after the customary civil marriage in the Town Hall

there could be a full marriage service in a Roman Catholic Church. No trouble or expense were spared to realize the hope. Prince Michael's private secretary, Sir Peter Scott, a former ambassador to Norway, travelled to and from Vienna and Rome seeing cardinals and other members of the hierarchy.

At first matters seemed to go smoothly. There were plans for a splendid wedding, no expense spared, with the internationally-famous Vienna Boys' Choir singing. Then Rome spoke. The Pope would give a dispensation for the Church marriage if, and only if, Prince Michael and Marie-Christine promised 'to do all in their power' to bring up any children of the marriage as Roman Catholics. Even if Prince Michael had been willing to assent to the condition, the Queen's advisers were against it on the grounds that it would be seen – and criticized – as the thin edge of the wedge of a Roman Catholic presence in the royal family.

That was that.

However, where there is wealth, power and influence something can generally be fixed. Sir Peter finally arranged for the civil ceremony to take place in Vienna and that on the following day Michael and Marie-Christine would attend mass at the Benedictine Priory, and a former Prior, Fr Pavlovsky, would administer the Holy Sacrament to her.

And this, finally, was what happened.

The royal family decided to make an appearance in force in Vienna to give open support even if Prince Michael was a relatively minor prince and his bride a divorced woman.

Lord Mountbatten, 'the centre of the family' as Prince Charles calls him, made the journey even though at seventy-eight he was looking frail. Princess Anne went. Prince Michael's immediate family attended – his elder brother, the Duke of Kent, with his daughter, Lady Helen Windsor, and his sister, Princess Alexandra with her husband, Mr Angus Ogilvy.

The royal family had not been pleased with the difficulties placed in the way of the marriage of Prince Michael and Prince Charles discovered that, fortuitously, he would be addressing the Salvation Army on the same Friday on which Prince Michael and Marie-Christine would be married at the Town

Hall in Vienna. He decided to do something about it.

Towards the end of a graceful speech honouring the Salvation Army's achievements he started a fresh theme:

'To my mind,' he began, 'the example set by the Salvation Army is Christianity at its most essential, simple and effective level, unfettered by academical or theological concern for dogma or doctrine. In an age when we are assailed on all sides by a host of outlandish philosophies and inhuman beliefs, when people are uncertain about what is right and what is wrong and anxious about being considered old-fashioned or out of date, it seems worse than folly that Christians should still argue and bicker over doctrinal matters which only serve to bring needless unhappiness and distress to a considerable number of people.'

The press, which normally would not pay much attention to a speech by Prince Charles to the Salvation Army, were alerted. The next morning it was headline news. 'CHARLES BLASTS CHURCH LEADERS', commented the *Daily Mirror*, alongside a story and picture of the Vienna wedding. 'THE FOLLY OF THE CHURCH – BY CHARLES' ran the headline of the *Daily Mail*, above the story, 'The new Princess forgets passport and rips dress.'

It was significant that the reason given for Charles's remarks was the Pope's decision to refuse a Church wedding to Prince Michael and Marie-Christine. It was largely ignored that Dr Coggan, the Archbishop of Canterbury, had refused to bend the rules of the Anglican Church and allow the couple to be married in one of the churches in his jurisdiction.

This was too much for some of the Roman Catholic hierarchy.

On the same day, Saturday, that Charles's remarks were published, Monsignor Thomas Winning, Archbishop of Glasgow, head of the city's 295,000 Catholic community, and an authority in Rome and Scotland on his Church's attitudes to marriage, made a robust statement: 'Perhaps Prince Charles should put his own house in order. You cannot have a Catholic on the throne of Great Britain, and the Prince cannot have a

Catholic wife. To do that he would have to abdicate. That is dogma too.'

He continued: 'His remarks will cause annoyance and anger to millions of the Queen's loyal subjects who place great store by truth, doctrine and moral principles, and who also care deeply about relations with their fellow Christians and other churches, and who still believe that matters of principle are important.'

Monsignor Winning was referring to the Bill of Rights of 1689 which firmly subordinated the monarchy to Parliament and on the subject of religion prohibited the possession of the crown to 'all and every person or persons that is, are or shall be reconciled to or shall hold communion with the See or Church of Rome or shall profess the Popish religion or shall marry a Papist.'

The Roman Catholics consider this an insulting relic of discrimination decreed at a time of religious dissension which has no relevance to the world of today.

An additional reason for Roman Catholic 'annoyance and anger', as Monsignor Winning put it, is that Prince Charles's remarks came at a time when the movement for reconciliation between the Church of England and the Church of Rome – the ecumenical movement – is finally showing signs of fulfilment.

The controversy did not end there.

The Times, edited by Mr William Rees-Mogg, a convert to Roman Catholicism, came out with a leader on the following Tuesday, July 4, headed, 'The Prince and The Pope'. Having explained the situation it said: 'The other principal question raised in the present controversy is the exclusion of a Roman Catholic from either being the sovereign or marrying the sovereign. As it stands, the unique exclusion in the law is an absurd anachronism. There can be no justification today for singling out the Roman Catholics in this way.'

In the same issue of the newspaper, however, Clifford Longley wrote (under the heading, 'The Time-Bomb Under The Throne'): 'Last January the Archbishop of Canterbury, Dr Donald Coggan, said in the Roman Catholic Cathedral in

Westminster that the time had come for Anglicans and Roman Catholics to receive communion from each other's hands. Good legal opinion has it that if the Queen herself were to follow his advice, she would immediately and for ever be disbarred from the Throne.'

The holiday season was approaching. Charles would be going to Balmoral. There would be grouse-shooting on the 6,700 acre moors of Delnadamph nearby which the Queen had earlier in the year bought for £750,000. There would be all the pleasures of a secluded country life that Charles appreciates. He might also be going to Iceland to share the splendid fishing with his friend, Lord Tryon, who has a lodge there.

But the controversy had given him much to think about – especially as he was friendly with Cardinal Hume and takes considerable interest in the ecumenical movement – and takes a favourable view of it.

In addition Charles and the royal family had to consider the implication of the divorce between the Queen's sister, Princess Margaret and Lord Snowdon which had been granted on 11 July on the grounds that the marriage had broken down.

The Queen and Prince Philip took Prince Andrew and Prince Edward to Canada at the end of July for the Commonwealth Games which opened at Edmonton on 3 August. Andrew, who had made a great success of his days at his Canadian school, Lakefield, was given his own dinner and dance in Ottawa at the official home of the Governor-General, Jules Leger. Most of the 120 guests were young people and Andrew was soon enjoying himself dancing with the pretty girls, including Lynn Nightingale, the twenty-one-year-old Canadian figure-skating champion. It was much the same story at Edmonton. Andrew enjoyed the events, talked with the competitors and spent a Saturday night at the city's best night-club, Darlings, dancing with the girls whilst the Prime Minister, Mr Pierre Trudeau, no mean swinger himself in his younger years, looked on approvingly. The Canadian press, radio and television enjoyed building him up as a handsome, extrovert, folksy prince. Andrew has made himself at home in Canada. He is just the sort of young man they like.

But it was noticed that Edward at fourteen was growing into a young man with even better looks than Andrew – or Charles – and that he bore himself with a certain grave dignity. It is as if Edward knows he has no need to impress people as Charles has to do, as heir to the throne, or Andrew by virtue of his personality. He will be his own man – and that is how he is developing at Gordonstoun. It has been said that he shows signs of being more aristocratic, more princely than either of his two older brothers.

Princess Anne was twenty-eight on 15 August and agreeable pictures taken by Lord Snowdon of her with her son, Peter, appeared in the press. She had been carrying out her duties this year with a certain consciousness that there had been criticism of her public attitudes and this tended to make her somewhat formal. But she and her husband, Captain Phillips, were spending a lot of time refurbishing their new country home, Gatcombe Park, and going the rounds of the horse events which were their main interest and where they had most friends.

At the end of August Prince Charles went to Nairobi to represent the Queen at the funeral of President Jomo Kenyatta, the father of independent Kenya. Another guest was President Amin of Uganda, whose actions in recent years have endeared him neither to Britain nor the world. Amin seized the hands of President Nyerere of Tanzania and President Kaunda of Zambia. Prince Charles was standing in the circle; but he turned away before Amin could grasp his hand.

At the beginning of October a significant appointment was made in Prince Charles's office which exemplified the power of tradition in the royal family. Mr Edward Adeane, thirty-nine, a libel lawyer, was appointed the Prince's private secretary with effect from May, 1979. His father, created Lord Adeane, had been the Queen's private secretary from 1953 to 1972. His great-grandfather, Lord Stamfordham, had been private secretary to Queen Victoria and George V. Squadron-Leader David Checketts who had been equerry and private secretary to the Prince for seventeen years was at forty-eight to leave to take up a public-relations job. Charles, it was said, was sad to lose his guide, companion and friend.

Adeane, educated at Eton and Cambridge, unmarried, was to inherit one of the most powerful posts in Buckingham Palace. It is no doubt intended that Adeane will be private secretary to the Prince throughout his years as heir to the throne and later serve him when he becomes King.

The post, as we know from memoirs of earlier years, is of crucial importance. The private secretary sieves carefully all the information that comes into his hands and then advises. In the hands of a diligent man this advice becomes difficult to neglect. Adeane has inherited generations of confidentiality and experience; he has proved his ability as a lawyer; he will, inevitably, play a considerable part in shaping Prince Charles's attitudes and influence what he says and what he does. It would be unwise to underestimate the ability of Edward Adeane or his capacity to work out on the chess board the necessary moves to preserve and enhance the position of the British monarchy and its Commonwealth titles in the future. But his background, an advantage in some respects, may make it difficult for him to appreciate what is going on at grass-roots level in the world. David Checketts was a Prince Philip man, unencumbered by protocol of the past. Edward Adeane has been born into that world.

Charles's office, apart from this appointment, is taking shape. His assistant private secretary is Mr Oliver Everett, thirty-five, who has been seconded from the Foreign Office. His press secretary is Mr John Dauth, thirty-one, who is on loan from the Australian diplomatic service. There is a duty equerry and two secretaries. To maintain his appearance the Prince has two valets. Other staff are drawn, when necessary, from Buckingham Palace.

With the help available from this organization, there was the question how Charles would best employ his time. The Queen has arranged that he should receive 'red boxes' from the ministries which enable him to acquire full information on certain subjects. Earlier in the year he had said in public that he wanted to acquaint himself with 'the whole spectrum of life in this country, with the world of industry, engineering, finance, agriculture and Government'. By acquiring this knowledge he hoped to be able to help Britain out of its downward spiral of industrial decline.

Now he got to know something about the National Economic Development Council and met trade union, management and government representatives on two of the sector working parties, concerned with electronics and transport. He had lunch with the Prime Minister, Mr James Callaghan, to discuss voluntary service among young people and the series of industrial visits he was to make. He was to join the board of the Commonwealth Development Council for three years from 1 January, 1979. This now operates in forty Commonwealth countries and dependencies and thirteen other developing countries. It has a budget of around £34 m and its present commitments on nearly 250 projects are about £370 m. Later in the year Charles spent two days at the Common Market headquarters in Brussels and saw Mr Roy Jenkins, the president of the E.E.C. commission, Mr Christopher Tugendhat, the Budget commissioner, Mr Gundelach, the agricultural commissioner with whom he discussed fishing policy, Vicomte Davignon, the industrial commissioner, and he talked about the United World Colleges with Mr Cheysson, the commissioner responsible for Third World relations. He then went on to visit N.A.T.O. headquarters.

All this activity was very valuable for the Prince. It was also valuable for the monarchy. His intelligent interest generated goodwill among men and women who are doing important jobs and who could be forgiven for thinking that Princes have little more than a decorative role to play in the modern world.

On the other hand, Charles is a very lucky man. His position gives him the privilege of meeting busy people who will, in his case, spare the time to discuss matters. Another example of this was the splendid trip to Yugoslavia organized for him by the veteran President Tito, at 86 the last survivor of the leaders in the Second World War.

Charles spent five days in the country from 23 October. He had lunch with Tito at his winter villa at Igalo and the Yugoslav leader, who had successfully defied both Germany and Russia, talked for nearly two hours about the war, about

Churchill, who gave him the vital backing he needed, about Yugoslav efforts to build a Communist state while preserving essential freedoms, about the present international situation. Tito has never forgotten that Britain was the first to recognize his efforts. He has paid three visits to England since the war and the Queen paid an official visit to Yugoslavia in 1972.

Charles toured some of the battlefields of the desperate struggle against the Germans and with him to explain what it had been like was Sir Fitzroy Maclean, who had been head of the British Mission at that time. There were visits to the Yugoslav navy, factories and industrial plants. He was helped by a series of beautiful interpreters and the mood of the trip was more than friendly – it was almost joyous. Charles was also lucky enough to be shown by an expert round the ruins of the great palace which that sagacious Emperor, Diocletian, built for his retirement. He was sagacious for he lived to enjoy some years there.

It was at this time that *Woman*, a magazine with a very large circulation, published the result of an opinion poll it had commissioned to gauge public support for the royal family. The most popular member was the Queen with 73 points out of 100. She was followed by Prince Charles, 61, the Duke of Edinburgh, 56, and the Queen Mother. Neither Princess Anne, nor her aunt, Princess Margaret fared well in the list. Indeed 45 per cent thought that Anne was arrogant.

The poll had also asked questions about Charles's choice of wife. Only 22 per cent said they would object if he married a divorced woman; only 14 per cent would object if he married a Roman Catholic and even less (6 per cent) if he chose a foreign princess. More than half said they would be content if he remained a bachelor.

Charles did not come back directly from Yugoslavia. He flew from Belgrade to Vienna and went to the estate of his friend, Prince Franz Josef of Lichtenstein, for a few days' shooting. He shot six wild boar which earned him the epithet of 'hooligan of the year' from an R.S.P.C.A. inspector, Mr John Bryant. Charles then flew on to West Germany and visited the 3rd Battalion of the Parachute Regiment at Osnabruck. When he arrived back in England he found that the Archbishop of Canterbury, Dr Coggan, had blessed the marriage of Prince Michael and Marie-Christine on 30 October at a private ceremony in Lambeth Palace. It has become a fairly normal practice for the Church of England to perform this service when divorce has made it impossible for the marriage to be held in church. Prince Charles may have thought that this marked the final end of the controversy of which he had been the centre earlier in the year. If so, he was mistaken.

He may well have been partly to blame for on 3 November he went back to Cambridge to give a lecture at the Union and answer questions afterwards. It was a serious lecture in which Charles tried to diagnose the ills of society, quoting extensively from Tolstoy, Baudelaire and Solzhenitsyn. Among the cures for the ills he made a plea for a more 'open-minded' approach to religious education. This was noticed and taken by some as a return to the theme of his Salvation Army speech.

Question time was lively as was to be expected with 700 undergraduates in the union chamber. He was asked, whether ironically or not, to explain his 'amazing success with women'.

He replied: 'I do not know how the idea has got about. The papers sometimes think I do. My constant battle is to escape. It is a very difficult problem. I often think my best way out is to announce my engagement to a Gladys Thrum. All the wedding presents would arrive and then I would call it all off and go about meeting all sorts of people. I don't think I have any great success at all. It must be because of who I am.'

The off-the-cuff remarks can be dismissed as inconsequential, except perhaps for his reference to his battle to escape which may have expressed a secret dream.

Charles was asked about his hunting and shooting and defended himself like a stag at bay, saying: 'Because you kill animals does not mean that you do not appreciate them fully and want to conserve them. I think if people did not partake in country sports in this country there would not be many animals left.'

He showed himself a romantic about the countryside, with no sympathy for modern farming methods – agrobusiness as it is called: Without country sports the countryside 'would be a basically average desert because most farmers would rather plough up hedges for more productive land.'

However, if Charles had a few problems at Cambridge, his sister Anne encountered worse when she went to Norway at this time to launch a fund-raising campaign for the 'Save The Children' organization of which she is president in Britain.

As part of her programme the Princess was to tour the children's wards of a hospital in Oslo, and the press expected to have normal facilities to take photographs and describe the scene. But the journalists found they were barred although a privileged television team was already inside. The Norwegians explained that it was nothing to do with them and that the instructions had been given by the British Embassy. When the television film was shown, it was severely criticized. Viewers were surprised when the Princess failed to shake the hand stretched out by a sick little boy. 'No cuddle, not even a smile', commented a front-page headline in the newspaper, *Dagbladet*. Another journal said it had received many telephone calls asking how a mother could show such lack of feeling.

The newspapers and news agencies made their protests about their exclusion to the British Embassy which made soothing noises. But the damage had been done – in a country which feels affectionate bonds link it with Britain. The trouble seems to have started with London warning the British Embassy that the Princess was not keen on the press. From that hint a desire to follow instructions had only escalated the trouble.

Charles's thirtieth birthday on 14 November fell on a Tuesday. From the previous Sunday the press carried long, carefully written articles by distinguished journalists recounting his life and explaining his activities with sympathy and considerable admiration. They echoed in varying degrees of intensity the remark Lord Mountbatten made about his great-nephew in answer to another admiral's exclamation: 'What a good piece of luck to have that young man as our next King!' 'Ah,' said Mountbatten, 'It's not luck at all, it's just a bloody miracle!'

On Monday evening Charles took Sarah Spencer to Covent Garden to see a gala performance of Meyerbeer's *L'Africaine* which was in aid of the Royal Opera House Benevolent Fund of which he is president.

On his birthday he was busy with the arrival of the President of Portugal on a state visit. He was among those who greeted him, lunched with the Portuguese and British suites in attendance and attended the state banquet in the evening at Buckingham Palace. In the afternoon, however, he went along to Regent Street to switch on the Christmas lights, cut a handsome birthday cake and listened for a short time to a choir singing carols.

On the next day, Wednesday, there was a big party for him at the Palace – 350 guests, a traditional dance band, a West Indian steel band and the Three Degrees, whom he had joined on the stage at the King's Country Club at Eastbourne in July during a charity night in aid of the Prince's Trust.

The birthday had passed – and Charles had not announced his engagement. But *The Times*, in adding its congratulations, did decide to voice what it called, 'sympathetic curiosity about his marriage plans'. It launched into the subject by saying: 'The list of eligible young ladies reared to the royal round who might win the Prince's heart is not long and is disproportionately long in Roman Catholics. He is, as the law stands, precluded from choosing a Roman Catholic bride if he and his heirs are to be eligible to succeed to the throne.' It continued: 'Many of the Queen's subjects who are not adherents of the reformed churches, and some of those who are, would consider this limitation on the Prince's choice, unnecessary, anachronistic, and very possibly irksome at this time.'

After suggesting that Parliament might amend the law and thus enable Prince Charles to marry a Roman Catholic, *The Times* ended by saying it would be unwise to make any moves unless Rome agreed in advance that it would not in such a case insist that the children were brought up as Roman Catholics.

Traditionally, *The Times* receives excellent information from the Palace so that these comments inevitably made people think that Prince Charles did indeed want to marry a Roman

Catholic and, realizing the legal barriers, was beginning to sound out opinion about the possibility of changing the law. This put his remarks to the Salvation Army in a different light.

There was news about Prince Andrew's future towards the end of November. He is to join the Navy for a twelve-year short-career commission starting towards the end of 1979 after taking his A-Levels at Gordonstoun. There was an element of surprise in the announcement for there had been strong rumours that he would go to Clare College, Cambridge. The college has high intellectual standards, but Andrew is bright and is expected to take three good A-Levels in English, History and Economics and Political Science. It would be possible for Andrew after initial training with the Navy to go under its auspices to university, but there are no plans at this stage. Andrew has grown into a tough, individualistic young man who may find it difficult to conform to naval traditions. But even a royal prince would find it hard to fight the system.

At the beginning of December Lady Jane Wellesley's name cropped up again for Charles went to the south of Spain for a partridge shoot on her father's estate and she was of the party. Scarcely was he back when Mr Enoch Powell made a sensational speech in which he said bluntly that both monarchy and nation would be in danger if he married a Roman Catholic.

Mr Powell, once a rising hope of the Conservative Party, now an intellectual gadfly whose bite goes deep, has established himself as a man of independent mind in the House of Commons and the country whose word carries weight. A fervent patriot and monarchist, his excellently-chosen words stir strong emotions.

He made his speech in his constituency of South Down in Northern Ireland where he sits as an Ulster Unionist M.P. He could not have chosen a more dramatic setting, for the Unionists are the staunch Protestants who still recall William of Orange in their name of Orangemen, and have since his time been locked in a bitter struggle with the Roman Catholic minority of Ulster.

Mr Powell opened by castigating those who pry into the private lives of the royal family to assert his moral rectitude and then launched into his diatribe against 'a hypothetical marriage' of Prince Charles with a Roman Catholic. After reviewing the historical background to the English break with the Church of Rome, he asserted that the issue was not so much religious as political and national. The break with Rome had enabled England to develop its independence. For Charles to marry a Roman Catholic the law would have to be changed and this would lead to a reconciliation between the Church of England and the Church of Rome which would subject the Anglican hierarchy to Rome.

Mr Powell then referred to the Common Market which he has opposed tooth-and-nail . . . 'For the first time since the Tudors another imperium, a superior external authority – judicial, fiscal and legislative – has been admitted.'

If the Church of England was destroyed as well, it 'would signal the beginning of the end of the British monarchy. It would portend the eventual surrender of everything that has made us, and keeps us still, a nation.'

This was a dire prophecy, made in all seriousness in a well-publicised speech. The question asked when he had spoken was, 'Why had he made the speech?'

The answer of Buckingham Palace was: 'We do not know why he has decided to raise this issue. All I can say is that Prince Charles is not engaged to marry anyone, let alone a Roman Catholic, and to the best of anyone's knowledge he does not intend to. Prince Charles is well aware of all the consequences of marrying a Roman Catholic, better than anyone. He knows that as the law stands he cannot marry one.'

The reaction from Rome was vehement. An executive official of the Secretariat for Christian Unity, said: 'My immediate reaction to Enoch Powell's speech is that I cannot see what sense it makes. In fact, it's utter nonsense. Is he really suggesting that the last bulwark of the Protestant establishment would be threatened if Prince Charles married a Catholic? It sounds silly to me. And worse still, it makes nonsense of the Christian unity drive.'

The speech, however, left an impression in Fleet Street and elsewhere of 'no smoke without fire', for Mr Powell is in receipt of information from many sources. The name of Marie-

Astrid of Luxembourg was recalled in spite of the emphatic denial of an engagement by the Palace following the *Daily Express* story of June, 1977. Palace denials have no great credence in Fleet Street – especially since the denial concerning Anne and Mark Phillips was followed swiftly by an engagement. It was also discovered that another Roman Catholic girl, Countess Angelika Lazansky, had spent a week-end at Balmoral in September, but there seemed little more to add.

It is difficult to be clear about what is going on. But it seems definite that something is happening. It may be that a campaign is about to be launched to remove the discrimination against Roman Catholics marrying into the royal family or reigning, solely to clinch a reconciliation between the Church of England and Rome. It may be that Charles does wish to marry a Roman Catholic and keep his right to succeed.

Before the Christmas holidays a final chapter ended the marriage of Princess Margaret and Lord Snowdon. The divorce was followed by the marriage of Lord Snowdon to Mrs Lucy Lindsey-Hogg, a television researcher he had known for some time, in a registry office on 15 December. There were no appeals to Archbishops and Cardinals in this case, just a sensible solution by sensible people arranging their relationships in a manner appropriate to the contemporary climate of opinion.

Anne's son, Peter Phillips, appeared on the television screen as part of the Queen's Christmas broadcast to stress her traditional theme of the importance of the family. At the New Year the family was, as usual, at Sandringham to spend a few weeks. Lady Sarah Spencer was invited for part of the time, so was her sister, Lady Diana, aged seventeen. Apart from being company for Charles and Andrew, they were there as a sympathetic gesture on the part of the Queen. Their father, Lord Spencer, who is a friend of the Queen and, indeed, the whole royal family, had a severe cerebral haemorrhage in the autumn and although he is only in his mid-fifties his life was in danger for months.

At Sandringham life was as normal during January. There was riding and shooting, good food and wine, talk and parlour games. But there was also television and the screens showed throughout January, 1979, a Britain suffering from snow, ice and fog and a series of industrial disputes, beginning with the transport drivers, which disrupted normal life and raised political passions in Westminster to unaccustomed bitterness.

Towards the end of the month, however, Charles went off for his usual skiing holiday with his friends at Klosters in Switzerland. His visit would probably have passed unnoticed if he had not fallen heavily on the ski slopes and had precautionary X-rays taken to see there was no damage. This was reported back in England. Normally, a skiing holiday by Charles evokes no particular reaction. But this year Britain was in an unusual mood . . . worried, beset by problems of getting to and from work, hampered by strikes and freezing weather, anxious about the basic necessities of life.

The Palace sensed that Prince Charles had been unwise to go off and enjoy himself under the circumstances and to silence criticism issued an unusually long statement giving details of his working plans for the months ahead. It was very impressive.

The Prince was to visit No 10 Downing Street on 13 February, sit in on a Cabinet economic policy committee, lunch with the Prime Minister and some of his ministers and then go to the House of Commons for Question Time. This was just one of seventy-seven engagements the Prince had arranged in the next six months. He was to make sixteen visits connected with industry, including a meeting with the Amalgamated Union of Engineering Workers and a trip on a trawler. He is to study the workings of the City, especially banking and insurance, and will address the Association of Head Teachers at their annual conference at Norwich in May. He will be visiting Hongkong, Singapore, Australia, Canada, France, West Germany and Denmark.

He has spent several days at Covent Garden making a film to be shown in aid of the development programme of the Opera House and will be laying the foundation stone of the first extension in August. He discovered there is an old foundation stone now embedded in one of the men's lavatories which he thinks ought to be used for it bears the name of another Prince of Wales – George, the Prince Regent, later George IV.

This was all very agreeable, but Charles is determined to show his interest in serious matters. He was to address the Parliamentary and Scientific Committee at lunch on 21 February and took a great deal of care with his speech.

The wave of strikes was still washing over Britain, and Fleet Street, predominantly Conservative in politics, had been whipping up opinion against the trade unions and generally painting a picture of a Britain in a state near anarchy. To a certain extent, it was the beginning of the general election campaign of 1979.

Charles began quietly enough: 'Anyone can emphasise the problems we face in this country – and without the slightest difficulty. Even without enthusiastic assistance from our partners in the E.E.C. or our transatlantic allies, we have become experts at the most destructive kind of self-denigration.' He then pointed out to get the record straight that, 'it is worth noting that an American survey, listing what were deemed major technical innovations around the world each year since 1953, found Great Britain to be the second largest source of such innovations – behind U.S.A., but well ahead of Germany, Japan, France and our other industrial competitors.'

He went on to stress the importance of increasing the numbers and status of engineers – a point which has been made often by leaders of industry. Then he came to his second point – the need to improve throughout our industry communications between the work-force and top management.

'But, somehow, something seems to have gone wrong with the system of communications in this country. People are not impossible to deal with. Unions are not impossible to deal with. Bloody-mindedness, if it arises, must do so surely, because of misunderstanding along the line.'

He spoke of his experiences visiting industry – how some managements seemed good and some bad – but he came out with an opinion very strongly: 'I have not the slightest hesitation in making the observation that much of British management doesn't seem to understand the importance of the human factor in the whole business.'

It was not a particularly controversial speech, but it annoyed some spokesmen for industry. Sir John Methven, the Director-General of the Confederation of British Industry, challenged the Prince to spend two or three years in industry, to experience at first hand the problems of low productivity, inadequate profitability, legislative intervention and the disincentive of high taxation. Mr Denys Randolph of the Institute of Directors, felt the speech was 'based on a rather superficial understanding of the problems.'

The *Daily Mail* printed an article by Mr Russell Lewis which said that Charles's speech had been 'thoroughly uninformed, unhelpful and one-sided.' The writer suggested that Charles had imbibed too much from Mr Callaghan and was risking going down into history as the 'Clown Prince'.

But Charles had his supporters. The *Daily Express*, the *Daily Mirror* and the *Evening News* came out in his favour.

Charles's speech could legitimately be criticized as somewhat superficial, but he had done his best to make a contribution towards solving the nation's problems. As the heat of the controversy died down, people became aware that they had a Prince of Wales who cared, who studied and thought and was willing to stand up and say his piece.

At the age of thirty Charles was beginning to create a new image. Not just a charming young man with girl-friends, polo ponies and a liking for music. He was beginning to make his mark as a new-style royal Prince who intends to involve himself in the real life of the nation.

The path has its dangers, but it could lead to a new concept of British monarchy in the world of tomorrow. Charles is showing the way with two younger brothers growing up to support him.

Conclusion

In the introduction stress was laid on the immense privileges to which the Queen's children were born, privileges almost unique in the world today. It has been suggested that these privileges could only be justified if the services rendered to the nation – and the Commonwealth – were of a special quality, such as the Queen has given.

In the succeeding chapters it has been possible to follow the pattern of life arranged for the Queen's children in their early years. As they have grown up Charles, Anne and Andrew have all expressed their views on many subjects and these remarks have also been recorded.

It is only natural to draw some conclusions, however tentative they may be.

Charles is the obvious centre of attention. He is heir to the throne and in November 1978 reached the age of thirty when a man's character begins to take on maturity. On the evidence available it seems fair to say that his life so far has been a success story. What makes it interesting is that the success has been hard won *by* him, not *for* him. Unhappy at school, not very bright at his books, disliking team games, he showed every sign of developing into a morose, withdrawn person of little apparent ability. What made this painful both for him and his parents was that the world was aware of it because his education had been public and well-publicized.

The change came during his six months at Timbertop in Australia when he was seventeen. He has said as much in his own words. It may have been that his body and mind needed a complete break with his former background to spark off a development that was almost a revolution.

He came back a different person. He believed in himself and started to make his own decisions – such as going to Cambridge. He was a success there; he was a success at Aberystwyth in difficult circumstances; his investiture as Prince of Wales and his subsequent tour of Wales was a considerable success.

He now began to speak his mind in the press, on the radio and television. He gave the impression of an intelligent, thoughtful young man, conscious of his responsibilities.

The five years in the navy could have been a bore to him and to the officers he was serving under, for the service is now so highly technical that it is difficult to carry passengers. But by choosing to become a helicopter pilot, a job not without hazards, he took on a specific duty which he could do well. By this and other challenges he has acquired a taste for danger.

All these years he was taking further opportunities to tell Britain, the Commonwealth and the world his views on life.

His relations with women have been a subject of world-wide interest ever since he was at Cambridge. He likes women, says so, and thus has increased his popularity with both men and women. There are, however, problems in an age of open reporting and comment. He has now had so many girlfriends and the roll-call has become so lengthy that it could become an embarrassment to his image. It is probably time that he settled down and got married.

It would be passing strange if the woman he marries is someone he has chosen for himself because he loves her. She will have to be acceptable to his mother, as Queen, to the government, other governments in the Commonwealth, and to public opinion generally. However permissive society may be in general terms, the bride of the Prince of Wales could probably not take on the task unless her background and life-style were as spotless as virgin snow. For the world press will investigate her pitilessly.

It is often asked what Charles will do during the years that stretch ahead as heir to the throne. The answer is what is he not going to do! He intends to follow in his mother's footsteps and do all he can to strengthen the Commonwealth. He is determined to do all he can to help Britain reverse its industrial decline and become a prosperous, united nation. In 1978 and 1979 he has been studying its financial and industrial situation, visiting factories, talking to management and trade unions, listening to the opinions of board-rooms and shop-floors, examining the relationship between government and industry in the modern world. He is already showing that he is willing to express his views in public, even if they do not please everyone. He is developing his knowledge and experience all the time. In addition to all this, he is finding time to be a patron of the arts, especially opera, and enjoys his polo, his fishing, his skiing and the companionship of his friends. He feels he has so much to do that is worthwhile. It is more than a lifetime's work.

Charles is proving that he is conscious of the duties of his position – and worthy of it.

If an able man is invested with all the trappings of power it is difficult not to believe that he has power. Charles appreciates that the British monarchy, deprived of direct power, has to rely on influence. But that influence, wisely used, can lead to a great deal of indirect power. This Charles also realizes as can be deduced from his own comments.

To gain and use this indirect power, both in the United Kingdom and the Commonwealth of which he will one day be Head, is a worthy ambition. To attempt to regain direct power, as George III, the ancestor he reveres, did successfully for a time, would be suicidal for the monarchy. This is not to say that the monarch, seeing the country faced with a totalitarian government of the right or left, might not stake all in measures to prevent this with the help of democratic forces in the country. If the attempt failed exile would be preferable to acquiescence.

This would be an extreme situation, hopefully never to be faced. But it is a situation that the monarch must have at the back of his or her mind. The monarchy has become the symbol of our freedoms as well as of our traditions of unity.

British institutions have survived by preserving ancient forms and changing their functions. The monarchy is a good example. The importance of monarchical influence depends

largely on the personality of the monarch. An able and indus-
trious man or woman, conscious of the absence of real power,
can by influence play a great part. The Queen is showing this.
Prince Charles shows many signs of following in her footsteps.
The challenge to strengthen the Commonwealth, in new terms,
is exciting and noble.

It would be pleasant to say that Anne has grown up into a
woman who is also conscious of her responsibilities. But there is
too much evidence, often provided by herself, that she finds
public life irksome.

Courage, determination and force of personality she has
shown. She is no fool and is conscious that her duty is to play
an important role. But it seems that she finds it impossible. Motherhood may change her. The years may mature her.
It may be that the Queen will decide that her daughter is un-
suited to her position and could do harm, rather than good to
the monarchy and the nation.

It would have a sad side, but Andrew and Edward are growing up. Both Andrew and Edward have had life easier than
Charles in their early years. The media have not taken the same
interest in them. They have been able to spend their years
without fear that their every action might be reported. Their
financial future is assured. Both are entitled to an allowance
of £20,000 a year from the Civil List when they are eighteen
and this will be increased to £50,000 a year when they marry.
These allowances can now under legislation passed in 1975
easily be adjusted to make them virtually inflation-proof.

Andrew has had a little publicity which has grown in the last
year or two because he has been expressing himself. A good
all-rounder, self-confident, very good-looking, he seems the
sort of young man who will take life in his stride. It might
be unwise to consider him as an integrated, extrovert character.
When he went to school in Canada in 1977 he said he hoped to
study drama because he liked to pretend he was someone else:
'I become bored with being myself and like taking on other
roles.' He added, 'My brother (Charles) is far better at dramatics. I make a comedian of myself.'

They are significant remarks. They show that under the

breezy confidence is the strain of being one of the Queen's children.

Edward is more like Charles when he was young – a quiet boy who likes fishing and bird-watching. He is quite bright and has charm. He now faces the challenge of Gordonstoun. Fortunately, like his brothers, he has a sense of humour to help him through.

Andrew is joining the Navy for some years at the end of 1979, but later if he has the talent and application he could devote himself to applied science, or, as it is now called, technology. A rejuvenated Britain needs new industries and a young and vigorous royal prince would be welcome to help in the many organizations which are trying to fit Britain for the future. He shows signs of the right sort of personality – direct and energetic.

As for Edward it would be splendid if he developed an interest in the arts. They are no longer the preserve of a small minority. Through education and the impact of radio and television the arts in the future have a chance they have not had for centuries to influence the lives of all. The opportunities for Edward would be boundless.

If such careers were followed by Andrew and Edward they would be following in the footsteps of their great ancestor, Albert, Queen Victoria's consort.

Such plans for the future can only be wishful thinking based on hopes that Andrew and Edward will want opportunities for careers which will fulfil them and strengthen the monarchy. Both boys have yet to develop. The results may be good or indifferent.

It is clear that Lord Mountbatten has exercised great influence on the royal family. It has probably been, on balance, a good influence. A man of great personal achievements in war and peace who has accepted change all his life, but tried to guide it in ways that would preserve what is worthwhile. In recent years Charles has grown close to him and found a wise counsellor.

If there is to be criticism of him, it is that he is too family-minded. The family is the great web of connections with the

German princely houses from which he and the royal family derive. His services to this nation have been great, as were those of his unjustly treated father, Prince Louis of Battenberg. For Lord Mountbatten, however, family is a source of almost obsessive interest. It is an attitude of mind shared by many others of less distinguished origin in many countries. In his case the effect is of considerable significance. He has considered it his duty to make the royal family conscious of their European connections in a way that could affect the deep-seated belief of the British people that the royal family is completely identified with it.

It is still hard to believe that it has been necessary to send all three sons of the Queen to Gordonstoun, even admitting that it has special qualities. It is a link with the German aristocracy, past and present, an aristocracy that has little or nothing to do with the new democratic post-war Germany with which Britain is so closely allied.

It has been an experiment for the Queen and Prince Philip to give their children an education away from home with other boys and girls. It had its risks, but they had to be taken as it is unlikely that in the present climate of opinion the children could have been brought up by governesses and tutors in the confines of the Palace.

Charles, Anne, Andrew and Edward now face the future. Their parents have done what they considered best for them. Their privileges are great. So are their responsibilities. They have a great heritage. Now it is up to them.

Index